Areté

ISSUE TWENTY — SPRING/SUMMER 2006

Areté

EDITOR: CRAIG RAINE
DEPUTY EDITOR: ANN PASTERNAK SLATER
ASSISTANT EDITOR: ADAM THIRLWELL

ADVISORY BOARD:
CARMEN CALLIL, DESMOND CLARKE, ANNA FORD, DAVID GODWIN,
CAROLINE MICHEL, ALAN RYAN, PETER STRAUS, CLAIRE TOMALIN

COVER DESIGN: RICHARD VAN DEN DOOL
DRAWING OF ARETÉ FEATHER: MARK ALEXANDER
WEBSITE: ELIZABETH STEWART

'The Greeks felt that areté was, above everything else, a power, an ability to do something. Strength and health are the areté of the body; cleverness and insight the areté of the mind.'

Werner Jaeger: *Paideia*

Areté, 8 New College Lane, Oxford, OX1 3BN, England
Phone: 01865 289193/ Fax: 01865 289194
e-mail: craig.raine@new.ox.ac.uk
www.aretemagazine.com
Unsolicited manuscripts should be accompanied by a stamped addressed envelope
© 2006 Copyright remains with the contributors
Areté magazine is registered as a limited company

Areté subscription information: see page 159

ISSUE TWENTY — SPRING/SUMMER 2006

APART FROM THAT	HAROLD PINTER	5
ON DIRECTING	PHYLLIDA LLOYD	9
SELF-DEFENCE	MATT CHARMAN	21
FOUR POEMS	OLIVER REYNOLDS	61
HOW TO REPAIR A QUILT	VERONICA HORWELL	31
A POEM	ALFRED CORN	43
TWO POEMS	ANDREW McNEILLIE	47
FLIES	IAN McEWAN	49
IN PREVIOUS EPISODES	FREDERIC RAPHAEL	81
WIFE OF BATH'S TALE	PETER SANSOM	93
IN GUATEMALA	VERONICA HORWELL	100
THE BROKEN WORD	ADAM FOULDS	119
'IT'S SYBILLE'	NICHOLAS MURRAY	136

Harold Pinter

Apart From That

Two people on mobile phones.

GENE
How are you?

LAKE
Very well. And you? Are you well?

GENE
I'm terribly well. How about you?

LAKE
Really well. I'm really well.

GENE
I'm so glad.

LAKE
Apart from ... oh you know ...

GENE
I know.

LAKE
Apart from ... oh you know ...

GENE
I do know. But apart from that ...?

LAKE
How about you?

GENE
Oh you know .... all things considered ...

LAKE
I know. But apart from that ...?

Silence.

GENE
Sorry. I've lost you.

LAKE
What do you mean?

GENE
I lost you.

LAKE
No you didn't. I'm right here. Where I was.

GENE
Anyway, where were we?

LAKE
Sorry?

Pause.

GENE
I mean apart from all that, how are you really?

LAKE
Terribly well.

GENE
Well you certainly sound well.

LAKE
I am. Apart from ... oh you know ....

GENE
Yes. I know.

LAKE
But *you're* well anyway.

GENE
I'm wonderfully well, to be honest

LAKE
I'm really glad.

GENE
Apart from ... you know ...

LAKE
But apart from that?

Silence.

GENE
What?

LAKE
Apart from that, how are you really? Apart from that?

Harold Pinter won the Nobel Prize for Literature in 2005.

Phyllida Lloyd

On Directing

In 1999 I was in preview for the musical *Mamma Mia* at the Prince Edward Theatre, London. This was the first blockbuster commercial show I had directed and the stakes were very high for everyone involved. Although the show had been developed painstakingly over some years and we had rehearsed it to within an inch of its life, it was a few days before our opening and still things were not working. The preview period is the chance to try a show out before an audience and improve it before the world's press descend and decide its fate. It is also the time, on a commercial venture such as this, with literally millions of pounds at stake, when everyone with a vested interest starts to have an opinion as to what should be done to improve it. As the director, whilst leaving no stone unturned to seek out the crucial changes, you also have to have nerves of steel and whilst appearing to hear everyone's opinion, disregard most of the advice you are given. It tends to fix on all kinds of things not at the heart of the matter. Like the curtain call or the colour of the leading ladies' hair. Our problems were in the first fifteen minutes of the evening. The audience was simply not with us and none of us could identify why. Every day we made changes. The cast were on a white-knuckle ride, often going in front of an audience with words they had been given only that afternoon. Then one day we decided to do something radical – to cut the whole of the opening musical number and replace it with new music and a new scene. We brought the actors in on

Sunday and on Monday went in with all guns blazing to show it to the audience. At the end of the show there was a certain amount of 'well done everyone, that has really helped !' but inwardly we were thinking, 'it has helped but has not solved our problems'. The next day I was approached by Andrew Treagus the general manager of the production. He said 'Phyllida, I am impressed by your tenacity but Thursday is our press night and I really must ask you for the sake of the whole company to make your final changes tomorrow...'

The next day I came in with a heavy heart and no new big idea. There was a letter for me at the stage door and I opened it as I made my way to the auditorium. It said 'Dear Phyllida Lloyd, I would not be writing to you if I did not know of your work for Opera North. You don't know me and you must throw this letter away if you feel it is impertinent of me to say that I saw your show two nights ago and I can see that you are in trouble. You have two scenes the wrong way round. You are trying to be something that you are not – a big blowsy Broadway show. You are an intimate domestic drama. Start with the plot and all else would follow. You have scenes a, b and c. Reverse b and c and you will not need a. Yours sincerely etc.' I sat down stunned for a second and knew what I had to do. But the producer was in a meeting, the writer was shopping in Knightsbridge for her first night outfit. The company of actors and an army of technicians were waiting for me in the stalls. I said, 'Ladies and Gentlemen, thank you for giving up your one day off to rehearse our new opening sequence. This is now cut and the show begins with the musical number "Honey honey!"' There was a look of dazed incomprehension on the faces of the cast – a sort of punch drunk, 'just tell us what to do and we will do it' – and a look of horror on the faces of the technicians at all the computer reprogramming of lighting and sound that this change would require. That night we tried our new version of the show. From the very first scene the audience were with us. We had been at the eleventh hour given our key. From that memorable experience and others like it less worthy of anecdote, I derive much consolation – that with enough training and an open mind, the solution will come but it may not come until the very last minute.

My first production, directing the worst actors I shall ever have to tolerate, was at my all-girls boarding school in the 1970s. This was a school where academic achievement was less important than learning to do the Charleston or make a damn good speech with which to open a church fete – or indeed to write and direct a play. This latter task fell to me for our annual play competition, held on midsummer eve on the Malvern hills. My working method – because, with this level of talent, that was all that one could resort to – was to be despotic and tyrannical, terrifying my actors, first into turning up, then into learning their lines and then speaking them louder and faster.

At university I was able to work with marginally better actors – at least ones who wanted to participate and ones who were less forgiving of a despotic regime. And this progression – from the start of one's career, with no craft under one's belt and slightly substandard actors, to gradually acquiring more and more skills and, one hopes, more and more talented actors with whom to collaborate – will allow one to relax one's grip on the tiller. To seek to empower the performer, not to cling to power oneself. Not to feel one has to solve all the problems in advance, not to be fearful if the solution does not come. It will come but maybe not until that last inch.

I have spent the last fifteen years working in both theatre and opera and I would like to share with you something of a life spent between these two worlds.

There was an American soprano, celebrated for her portrayal of Medea in Cherubini's opera of that name. In the opera Medea sings her final aria and leaves the stage to murder her children. This formidable diva had sung the role in French all over Europe and was to sing it for the first time in America in English. At the *Sitzprobe* the conductor said 'let's miss out number such and such and go from just before she leaves to kill the children.' The woman threw down her score and let out a stupified shriek 'she kills her children ???!!!'

Apocryphal though this story might be, opera at its worst is an antediluvian, unwieldy medium. The director is up against it if searching for ideal conditions in which to work. In international opera – and I mean opera where the star singer is the be all and end all of the event – the stars are not paid to rehearse. The process of rehearsal is stolen, compromised, often a fiasco. The product is all. But look at it from the singer's point of view – why should they come for more than a week in the rehearsal room when they've probably done the role before in another production and, besides, they might earn £10000 a night for a couple of concerts the week before?

I have waited for a week for a leading singer to arrive – each day them phoning in sick – only to find they are indeed singing concerts in another European capital. When they do arrive they may be astonishingly lacking in intellectual curiosity. Even those with the curiosity can only afford to be so curious. If they've done four other productions of *Rigoletto* they can only become so involved in your dreams. And how can they afford to keep arriving at first rehearsals with a probing interest in the set and costume design when so often they are stepping into dead mens' shoes in productions that may be over 30 years old? At worst they are hired for what are known as their money notes – usually high ones – they may know those notes but be oblivious of what anyone else on stage is singing to them. If they need to know when to sing, the conductor will wave his stick. If they don't know what to sing, a little lady – and she must be little for she is in a small box buried in the stage – will shout out their next line in the bar before they need it... And so if the singer on stage with you forgets to sing you the question, it doesn't matter if you are not listening. Someone will tell you what to answer.

Once the singers have arrived – and God knows whether you will ever see the right people in a scene in the room together – you may get to meet the conductor. He might breeze in, expect to be called *maestro*, look at the scene that you have worked for some days to carefully organise – and demand that, for 'musical reasons', everyone ignore what they have rehearsed, come down to the front of the stage and sing out to the audience.

And then there's the chorus – like trying to direct your parents. In Paris they may down tools at any moment for a union meeting. They may tell you on day one that for health reasons they may be unable to kneel, unable to touch each other because they are allergic to the washing detergent in each others' skirts, get a wobbly feeling if asked to walk clockwise on a raked stage.

Try creating an intimate atmosphere in the rehearsal room with fifteen of you there sitting behind tables like a panel of judges. And as for an ensemble, how could one hope to create that when the star singer is being paid literally 50 times the wages of say a dancer on the show?

Then if you have by a miracle managed to create something which gives you hope, this game is more precarious than training horses for the Derby: you must face the fact that it is highly possible that on your first night one of your leading players will have contracted a sniffle and will cancel.

So why would one work in this medium if one could work in the theatre?

Last year I directed Schiller's remarkable play *Mary Stuart* about Elizabeth I and Mary Queen of Scots. The actress Janet McTeer and I had worked together several times and wanted to again. We looked for a play and a theatre suggested this play and that Janet should play Mary Stuart. We developed the project over six months before starting rehearsal. We commissioned Peter Oswald to translate it and Anthony Ward to design it. We had six weeks of rehearsal. Each of the actors was paid the same wage and though some had more lines than others and up to 40 years' more experience, by the time we opened, the best ideas were coming from the boy in his first job.

Here the actors not only turned up on time, they were embarrassed to be ten minutes late – let alone a week. And as for cancelling a performance – they would have to be unable to speak or walk. They came mentally prepared, with baskets of research, already critically involved at the presentation of the set and costume design on day one – that is, if they had not already contacted me months before asking to talk about the play, to hear about my ideas. They may not know their lines on day one, but God knows they come ripe and ready. They know that on the night there will be no safety net – no conductor to tell them when to speak, no prompt to tell them what to speak, no one to tell them *when to end the silence*. They may have a play in verse or prose and it will have its internal rhythm but they will have to decide when to play across that rhythm, they must choose the tempo. It's all down to them. And this makes them sharp. It makes them need, above all, each other. It makes them listen. And acting is listening. Because from the listening is born the speaking. And this is what makes it harder to produce a great production of a play than a great production of an opera. Because, in the theatre, the director must arbitrate on rhythm and tempo. In opera Verdi and the conductor largely take care of that.

So the director's quest will be to create an ensemble that can play in concert. To make each of the eleven feel safe to be as dangerous as they must be on stage – and that will mean doing whatever is required to bring each person, each scene to the point of readiness. And that might mean different things for each actor. One thinks that improvisation will release the scene – another that she is so old she can barely learn the lines she has, let alone improvise them. And this is a play set in two worlds – the court of Elizabeth I and the prison of Mary Stuart. A Catholic world and a Protestant world. And it soon became obvious to me that each of the actresses, each of the queens, was building their own courts, their own worlds. Crudely, there was the court of the mind and the court of the heart. And the court of the mind rehearsed with forensic attention to detail – using techniques on the text such as actioning each line of the text. So that a line such as 'who was that speaking?' would be explored at first as a challenge, then an accusation, then a tease and so on. Meanwhile in the court of the heart there was improvisation, rawness and chaos. The difficulty came when we rehearsed the great and fictitious scene in which the two queens meet. The court of the mind needed to analyse and steady the process, the court of the heart was impeded by the cold scrutiny, aching to 'just try something'. Now all great acting is a synthesis of mind and heart but each of the actresses was moving towards their goals from different poles. As the work went on, the court of the mind allowed more passion and chaos into its borders, whilst the court of the heart began to focus, edit, and balance. None of this can be premeditated on the part of the director. The trick is to keep one's mind open enough to be able to see and hear it and draw on one's craft to organise it.

And all the time the actors are closing the gap between themselves and the text – I mean owning the text as if no one has ever spoken it before. There are changes daily, as new fragments of translation arrive by email, cuts are made, transpositions are suggested. The whole event is intimate, there are thirteen of us in the rehearsal room – everyone has a voice. And the root of it is that everyone turns up. And everyone spends the TIME it takes to make the work work.

So why would I direct opera? Because when the conditions are right, to be a part of that massive collaboration with 80 musicians in the pit and 100 on the stage is to be part of something much greater than oneself, to help to give the audience a raw emotional experience like no other. Opera operates on a subterranean level and can reach parts of you that other art forms really do struggle to reach. Opera is an event. Performances are at a premium, a production prepared over several years may have eight performances only. And to collaborate with great acting singers such as I have had the fortune to do – ones of such skill, such fearlessness, such a marriage of astounding technique and full blown passion, such a preparedness to fall from a great height, such ambition for the possibilities of this unwieldy medium – has been one of the blessings of my professional life. And in this country it is still possible to find those ideal conditions in which to work.

About eight years ago I was called in to the director's office at English National Opera and asked 'do you ever listen to Wagner?' I replied 'not much, no'. 'I think you should start', said my boss. 'Where?' I asked, thinking I was going to be asked to direct a recently excavated and hitherto unperformed piece of Wagnerian juvenilia. 'I'd have a listen to the *Ring*', he said. Now *The Ring* is sixteen hours long. You need to take a short holiday just to get through it. This vast saga – which had not been performed in England in English for 30 years, and had maybe only once ever been directed by a woman – is the most gigantic project that any theatre company will undertake. And the unthinkable had happened. I was being asked to direct it. It was as surreal as if someone had said to me 'you will now go and work for five years in a field hospital in Rwanda'. It seemed that much of a change of direction, that much of a bracket round the rest of my life. I had four years to cast it, work with a designer to create the sets and costumes and find someone to translate it. For the text in English was to be the be all and end all of this endeavour.

It was like preparing a gigantic banquet, a banquet that was to be marinaded and slow cooked over a long time. And I didn't worry that parts of the piece remained foreign to me for several years, because to this piece above all there could be no ultimate solution. Each director must simply choose his or her path through the forest of it and hope to lead others with them. With time and an open mind the way through the woods would emerge.

Now this experience was the opposite of everything I have outlined about international opera and the key to it all was TIME.

The rehearsal process for companies such as English National Opera is still sacred. People are paid to do it and the singers, who may well spend other parts of their lives in the international opera of which I spoke so disparagingly, turn up and turn up every day. They may not all arrive with the same sense of query and interest in the whole that a group of actors bring, but with time they develop it.

So though this *Ring* adventure would have seemed as far away from an experience like *Mary Stuart* as it was possible to imagine, one could proceed, not just with the staging of the piece – and believe me the staging is the easy bit – but with the exploration, the process. One had time.

But how do you actually work with singers if you have the time to do more than the staging? What do you physically do?

Of the nine months I spent in the rehearsal room with Wagner, a considerable amount of time was spent without music – to try to get the singers to listen to each other, so that their listening was as interesting as their singing and their singing only came because of what they had heard. The *Rhinegold* is the first of the four operas. It's a brilliant family saga in which a man sells his sister-in-law to his builders in settlement of the bill for the house they have constructed for him. Love is sacrificed for political power – there are no arias, barely any ensembles of singing – it's more like a play set to music. Early in the process I asked the singers to make a circle and, speaking their lines of text, throw a football on the last word of each of their lines to whom they thought they were communicating. Firstly, even though they knew their music backwards, without it, they not only didn't know their words but they often did not know when to say them or to whom they were talking. Then, once we had established precisely who was doing what to whom and when, I took away their text and asked them to improvise scenes, to make up the words – and then they stopped worrying about where they were standing and when to move, and began to inhabit the action in three dimensions. The quest was to get them to own the experience, to begin to take responsibility for more than just their bit.

Gradually over the weeks they began to become interested in each other, and very demanding – 'could you make eye contact with me please?' 'What are you trying to do to me with that phrase of music?', 'I just don't feel anything is happening ...' And as the months passed, we rehearsed the next opera, and the next, and they began to take responsibility for matters beyond themselves – to call me late at night with ideas for the following day, to arrive at rehearsal with reams of cuttings from the newspapers, stories that collided with what we were doing. And this was not just the singers. The stage management team would come in on Monday morning and say 'we met for a drink yesterday and discussed the transformation of the man into the toad. We think we have a solution.'

And the conductor – far from turning up at the last moment – would be present at these sessions and I would attend his music rehearsals and we would together with the translator Jeremy Sams to hone and refine the translation of the text. This was a massive collaborative effort.

It is not just its principal singers who, with time, one can work in just the way one would with an actor. It's the chorus, too. And an opera chorus at the height of its powers is one of the wonders of the world. Working with them one of the theatre's great challenges and privileges.

At Opera North in Leeds it was a hot Friday afternoon in the rehearsal room and the chorus would rather have been at the Test Match up the road at Headingley. The chorus master had suddenly had enough of their restive behaviour. He uncharacteristically put down his baton and threw (to put no finer point on it) a complete wobbly. He began screeching at them that they were desecrating the shrine of one of the great composers of the Nineteenth Century, riding roughshod over all that they had prepared, undermining their profession, insulting him, ruining the work for the principal singers and this tirade seemed to go on and on until he simply had to pause for breath and a tweed jacketed tenor pulled a transistor radio earpiece from his ear and said, 'Botham's out!'

The chorus is the great leveller. They are the man or woman in the street who can sniff out the pretentious or the fake at 50 paces. They are often rehearsing four operas at once so you have to earn your stripes and not expect them to make your production the centre of their world on day one. But make it the centre of their world they will – and will go out on an opening night as if their lives depended upon it. Above all they like to be treated as individuals. They like to collaborate.

So when four months into our *Ring* cycle rehearsals, we were invited to the Glastonbury rock festival to sing the last act of the *Valkyrie*, after James Brown and before Paul McCartney, in front of an audience of 40,000, we were very very excited and very very nervous... What would the audience think? This moment in the drama comes about five hours into the evening and, after the famous ride of the Valkyrie start, comes one of the stillest and most intense two handed scenes in the whole of opera. Would they start to slow hand clap or drift away to the beer tent? But the audience not only stood rapt, they shouted ' shoosh' when a mobile phone rang in the crowd, and 'leave her alone you pervert !' when Wotan threatened to cast his daughter Brunhilde out of his world for ever, and burst into applause when he appeared to reprieve her – and would not let the cast off the stage at the end. This had much to do with the genius of Wagner but something also to do with the fact that the singers, taken quite out of their natural element, had taken so much time in the preparation, and were so utterly convinced of who they were and what they were singing that they went out there with the confidence and brio of rock stars.

And when the critics sporadically took pot shots at us – and a critical mauling for Wagner, it has to be said, is a badge of honour in some circles – we felt as if roped together on a precipice of Everest – on an expedition, so long in the planning, so gargantuan, so exhausting, so exhilarating, that the outraged cries of the critics were like voices down in a village somewhere far away calling to us, trying to get us to look down. But they had no power to divert us from our task.

Five years ago I was working in New York City directing my first Broadway Musical. I left my apartment at 0900 hours and the doorman said 'a plane just went into one of the twin towers'. By the time I emerged from the subway at Union Square there was a huge crowd in the street staring in horror at the World Trade Center now engulfed in black smoke. Two hours later both towers had collapsed. I had a cast of actors, some of whom were less than twenty years old. They were Canadian and away from home for the first time. Canada is a country that has barely had a shot fired in anger on its home ground. They had closed the island of Manhattan to the outside world and we were on it. People were crying and terrified. Two days later we gathered together to speak of where we were and how we should proceed. Some said we should make sandwiches for the firemen, others that we should go straight away and give blood. One said whatever we do we can't do 'this' – meaning the job in hand, our job, to rehearse a musical. A more experienced member of the company said, 'But this is what we do. Some people flip burgers, drive subway trains. Or are nurses. This is what we are trained to do. They may not need us now but the time will come when they do and we must be ready.' I don't think I have ever felt more responsible for the next steps taken in a rehearsal room – how we as a group were to conduct ourselves and how I as the leader of that group was to proceed. Five weeks later we were the first show to open on Broadway.

Can theatre change the world? I'm not sure, but it can provide consolation in grief, a roar against injustice or an evening of downright silliness. And it would be perverse if how we created it, the process by which we worked, were not at least as important as the end result – were not a reflection of how we wanted the world around us to be.

Phyllida Lloyd is the Cameron Mackintosh professor of Drama at the University of Oxford. This is the text of her inaugural lecture delivered on 5 March 2006.

Our Böld

Hearing Aid

In Seamus Heaney's introduction to *Poet to Poet: W B Yeats*, there are passages which baffle us by their banausic obnubilation. We are reminded of Vladimir Nabokov's slighting summary of George Steiner's tribute to himself – Nabokov, not Steiner: 'solid abstractions and opaque generalisations'.

It is Heaney's view that 'Poems in which the defiant self is pitted against hostile or disabling conditions – "An Irish Airman Foresees His Death", "September 1913", "Meditations in Time of Civil War" – are complemented by poems that read like discharges of pure, self-possessed energy, poems from which the accidental circumstances have been excluded, **so that all that remains is the melody and stamina of resurgent spirit...**'

Even blether:

'The speculations of *A Vision* (1925) and the poems of *The Tower* (1928) and *The Winding Stair and Other Poems* (1933) **have a planetary range and splendour, and incorporate haphazard yet powerfully registered incidents of personal and public life within the orbit of a single, ardent intelligence.**'

Seeing stars?

But we think there is an explanation. Some of the prose seems to be translated from German.

For a finale, Heaney serves up a take-away from Rilke's first 'Sonnet to Orpheus': 'da schufst du ihnen Tempel im Gehör.' We call this tripling your spells. Or should that be *Spiels*?

'Yeats's essential gift is his ability to **raise a temple in the ear, to make a vaulted space in language through the firmness, in-placeness and undislodgeableness of stanzaic form.**'

Matt Charman

Self Defence

A girl in her mid-twenties, Nia. We get the sense she's been sitting for sometime. As she remembers thoughts, she speaks them, almost as quickly as they come into her head.

NIA

[*Number one*]

We borrowed an eight year old to come and stay for the weekend because Neil said it was the toughest age to control and it would therefore be the best test of whether we had 'parental instincts' or not. [*Beat*] I reminded him of the period in a child's life known as the 'terrible twos' but he said it was a fallacy that kids were any trouble at two and that it's actually at eight years old that the cracks begin to show in a child's personality.

    Neil called it a road test and even though I asked him not to I still heard him refer to it as a road test to his brother on the phone. The kid was called Isaac and we picked him up on a Saturday morning from a colleague of Neil's. I was hoping for a little boy who didn't say very much and was nervous, whose life we could have a huge impact on in one day. [*Beat*] In fact he was very talkative and quite dominating conversationally. Neil was certain by the time we got home that he and Isaac were incompatible and that this wouldn't be a fair trial of his parental skills. He asked whether I would mind if he observed me with the child instead to see if I had what it took to be the parent of a difficult eight year old, something he foresaw as a worse case scenario. [*Beat*] I was terrible with Isaac. Aware Neil was watching me from the lounge I allowed the child too much autonomy in the kitchen and he cut his hand with a vegetable knife.

[*Number two*]

739 people a year are injured by watering cans. 431 by clothes pegs and 493 by cakes or scones.

[*Number three*]

It took us five attempts to get the answer machine message right when we first recorded it. I wrote it out and underlined Neil's part because I wanted us to each say a bit of the message so what people heard when they called was both of us together in our home. When you consider that some people don't change their answer machine messages until they change their actual phone then it might be that a message is used for three or four years so it's worth getting it right initially.

Neil calls from work when he thinks I'm not in, to hear my voice on the answer machine and then he hangs up. I dial 1471. Ali won't leave a message on the machine because she says she hears Neil's voice and it doesn't feel private.

[*Number four*]

Ali my sister who is a year younger than me and from a different father, is a Gemini. She's independent and classically difficult to be around. Her and Neil have never got on well and had a fight on our third wedding anniversary about whether we should celebrate wedding anniversaries at all. I sided with Neil because I happen to agree with him that celebrating anniversaries is an important testament to fidelity and longevity in a society where more people fall apart now than stay together. Ali has a difficult streak and has never liked Neil. She said to mum when I got engaged, don't expect me to marry a man like Neil and she meant it. She brought Steve to our wedding instead who had a tattoo on his hand of three little dots shaped in a triangle. At the reception Steve told Neil that he was an idiot for settling down at such a young age and then he pointed at the dots on his hand and said it was his mantra: 'Find them, Fuck them, Forget about them'. Neil said he didn't have a mantra so Steve borrowed a biro and drew three dots on his hand and said 'Now you have'. Neil washed them off and told me all about it. Steve took money from my sister before he disappeared which must have been difficult because she didn't have any. Mum died and Ali said it's just you and me now.

[*Number five*]

I told Isaac over lunch 'not to lick your knife you fucking little pig' ... I wanted to tell him that. I didn't tell him that. His little plaster started to bleed. I'm worried I'd hurt our baby.

We took Isaac to the cinema in the afternoon because he wouldn't go bowling because of his asthma. We watched a film with Johnny Depp in it, which both Isaac and I loved and bonded over on the way home. Neil watched me in the rear view mirror, impressed with the rapport I was building with Isaac I think.

[*Number six*]

A few months ago when Neil got a little bit fat because we're contented and I'm aware that happens to couples, I used a screwdriver and took the bathroom scales apart. With the stickers you get when you buy a blank video I changed the numbers on the scale so that 13 stone now read 14 stone. Neil soon became concerned at his weight gain and we designed a diet together, which proved successful. When he began losing weight I moved the numbers again, as the ideal weight for Neil's height is actually ten and a half stone and I knew he would get down to eleven stone then stop. When he reached ten stone I adjusted the scales so they now read twelve stone. I got him down to nine and a half stone with this method, which is I realise, technically a stone underweight for Neil but I thought it was probably a good thing for his all round health.

[*Number seven*]

While I walked, out the corner of my eye I saw a street performer juggling fire along by the river. I stopped and watched him because it was getting dark and the flames looked impressive at dusk. A crowd gathered and he sent these sticks up higher and higher until one got away from him and landed in the hood of a girl in the crowd who was a tourist. The flame from the stick didn't burn for long because it's designed not to but it still burnt her pony tail and all up the back of her neck was blistered. People hung around and waited until an ambulance came and the whole area stunk highly of singed hair. The performer waited as well, feeling terrible and making conversation with people. When the ambulance came I went.

[*Number eight*]

Ali went abroad which I found out from a postcard she sent me. She was in Thailand then a month later she was in Cambodia. She said she gave up her job and e-bayed everything for her ticket including things I'd lent her which I thought was a joke but might have been true. I don't use e-bay I don't know.

[*Number nine*]

Don't get business cards printed from a machine in a service station even if they're in colour. Neil did when he lost his job and it held him back for weeks. He was stubborn and he wouldn't admit that the card was thin and cheap and that the font wasn't sophisticated enough for the responsibility level he was applying for. He said the card was more 'a tick in a box than anything' and the quality of it really didn't matter much but if that's what you leave behind in people's hands after an interview then the quality matters most of all. It's like the aftertaste of something, I said. It doesn't matter if you've enjoyed the meal, in this case the interview, if the aftertaste, in this case the card – is bad, if the card is bad it makes you re-appraise the meal, the interview. We rowed a lot about that.

[*Number ten*]

They drilled open the lock on a flat in Bethnal Green and found a pile of post dating back to December 2004. Ali was in arrears with her rent and they wanted to kick her out. I didn't even know she was back in the country. Inside the television was on and Ali was laid out on the carpet by a homemade Christmas tree with presents underneath. All the bulbs except two had burnt out on the Christmas tree lights because she'd been lying there like that for eight months and it was summer now. They used her teeth to identify her.

[*Number eleven*]

Late in the afternoon when I was bored of talking about Johnny Depp and Isaac seemed to be slowing down Neil joined us at the table. He had a suggestion for a game that wouldn't aggravate Isaacs breathing but that might be more boisterous and therefore boyish compared to the low-key activities we'd done till now, which were his words. The 'men' went outside and while I pretended to be casual about it I rushed upstairs to look at them from the bedroom window. Neil began by showing Isaac our small garden and how to re-pot a plant.

[*Beat*] Neil was good with Isaac. He was encouraging too with a tone of voice I'd never heard him use before. A little bit like when we move furniture together but less patronising. I realised then Neil could make a good father and that the road test had been a good idea. Isaac got wheezy and had to stop but it didn't change my feelings of how Neil had handled their half an hour together.

[*Number twelve*]

The lonely deaths officer asked me if we were a close family, Ali and I. I had to say no. A lonely deaths officer is a horrible job title. It's hard to think of a worse one.

[*Number thirteen*]

We returned Isaac to his parents' house that evening. I didn't get a glimpse of his father but I waved at his mother who waved back. We drove home pretty contented, Neil and I. We talked about it in bed. How it had all gone. Neil had warmed to Isaac but he still didn't altogether trust him although he realised that wouldn't be an issue with his own baby. [*Beat*] Lightning strikes, Neil said, the same spot some times. The things that happen aren't my fault. I can be a mother. He said that and then he switched off the light.

[*Number fourteen*]

Curtain pelmets injure 129 people a year.

[*Number fifteen*]

No one should lie there for eight months without anyone knocking on the door especially not my sister. She said I was trapped but I think it was her who was trapped because everything disappointed Ali. Nothing lived up to her expectations. She left a pile of clothes and the two books she was reading, one of which had a Frog in the title and a bunch of unprocessed film that I knew would be of her because she loved taking photos of herself with the camera I gave her second hand after Neil made the switch to digital. People handle things differently. You can dig a hole and bury yourself in it, not just your head your whole self or you can choose the opposite direction which I did and she found laughable. I don't care. I'm right and she's wrong because I'm still here. I wouldn't have laid there for eight months without anyone in my life finding me. Neil would have found me or our baby would.

[*Number sixteen*]

I sat on the bus in the pregnant seats. I sat behind a girl with a scar on her neck and short hair and I wanted to tap her on the shoulder to see if she was the one who got burnt that night by the river. I always thought she was a tourist and that she'd probably gone back by now but maybe she was foreign and lived here all along. I like the idea that she stayed. I hate the idea that she went home and had to explain the scar and her singed hair to people. She survived. That's the main thing.

Matt Charman's first play *A Night at the Dogs* which won the 2004 Verity Bargate award was performed at the Soho Theatre in April 2005. He is writer in residence at the Soho Theatre and is currently on attachment at the National Theatre Studio.

Oliver Reynolds

Four Poems

A History of the Latrine from Herculaneum to London

Appolinaris medicus
Titi imperatoris
hic cacavit bene

Dixon – Doctor
to George III –
here took the throne
and left this turd

Gents

According to Constable Keen
both men clearly wanted
    to linger:

his torch had shown
each giving the other
    the finger.

Top C

Did this shy soprano
    mean to

have her introitus
    seen to

in the under-gardener's
    lean-to?

Eighteen Geo. II. c. 27

Every Person or Persons
who shall by Day or Night feloniously steal

any Linen, Fustian, Callico, Cotton, Cloth,
or Cloth worked, woven, or made of any Cotton
or Linen Yarn, mixed, or any Thread, Linen or Cotton Yarn,
Linen or Cotton Tape, Incle, Filleting, Laces, or any other
Linen, Fustian, or Cotton Goods, or Wares whatsoever,

laid, placed, or exposed to be printed,
whitened, bowked, bleached, or dryed,

in any whitening or bleaching Croft,
Lands, Fields, or Grounds,
Bowking-house, Drying-house, Printing-house,
or any other Building, Ground, or Place,

made use of by any Callico Printer,
Whister, Crofter, Bowker, or Bleacher,

for Printing, Whitening, Bowking,
Bleaching, or Drying of the same,

to the Value of the ten Shillings,

or who shall aid or assist,
or shall wilfully or maliciously
hire or procure any other Person or Persons
to commit any such Offence,

or who shall buy or receive
any such Goods or Wares so stolen,
knowing the same to be stolen as aforesaid,

shall on conviction be deemed guilty of Felony
without Benefit of Clergy

and be punished with Death.

Oliver Reynolds is the author of four collections of poems: *Skevington's Daughter* (1985), *The Player Queen's Wife* (1987), *The Oslo Tram* (1991) and *Almost* (1999), all from Faber.

Veronica Horwell

How to Repair a Quilt

My room was downtown in LA. A sixth-floor room at the side; not even the LA parking lots were full around the hotel, though their borders were dense double-parked with woody weeds. There was a lump under a blanket on the sidewalk below, broken shoes showing; the derelict was not dead, he roared up if you passed too close, but as the afternoon faded he lay prone. Eastwards, over tarmac, was a Broadway which still had picturehouses from the first days of the Kinema – greasy dirt thick on stone roses, on terrazzo inlays replacing the paving like a permanent carpet for a premiere. Westwards, there were banks, offices built a year or two before the movie people came: built Babylonian, and built in that especial American Roman, with its shallow bronze bowls for electric lights. Rich. Griffiths's *Intolerance* set must have been just a plaster oversizing of the decor of the banks and moving picture houses of his period.

But most of my prospect was the blank wall of the depository across the lot, and – something to watch – there was lighting-up time at the Bunker Hill towers up the safer end of the road. They were the *LA Law* credits: that one with triple blue fours, the Four-Four-Four, was *the* office block. Only they were not dressed overall in internal neon as on film. Several floors went missing into darkness, and there was a different configuration of blanks nightly. But still plenty of gassy blue colour-washed the room. That night I spent in. I had a beer in Hank's bar down in the lobby, an early beer, just Big John, the quiet vet barman from Wyoming, and me. Too early to trade Churchill quotes with the joint's owner, an old guy whose face as a dapper bantam fighter I could see on a memorial board behind the till: he was standing behind his wife, a classy dame of the Bacall era. There was another picture of her alone on some boulevard under palms. 'You are beautiful, you are loved eternally,' said the words. She had died a few months back.

It was a regulars' bar, hung with flags and photos of cops around drugs-bust bags. The laundry service van driver drank there, and a silver-haired corporate lawyer from 444. 'The Way We Were' was always on the juke and the game, any game, on the screen. I drank, not too much, not too often, and kept on my limewashed sombrero, because it made me safely an outsider. I could get tacos from the coffee-shop across the lobby, nodding politely in passing to the Sikhs who ran the hotel, which put up old men and midwest kids. But the diner was closed that day. And the waiter – who had said one morning that he understood when he saw me crying – was not home. He was here and his family were somewhere else, and his heart was swollen and burnt, he said. Mi Corazon. Behind the closed door the waitress was hanging up baby shower signs in Spanish. I wasn't foodless, I had a bag of the new crop's golden raisins in my room, and a quart of ginless lime rickey from a stall in the city market. Stall, too improvised a word: a juice fountain. It dispensed health drinks from chrome tanks, their names lettered on old plastic slot-ins. Its laminate counter was old, too, and the enamelled blenders that smashed up the fruit: it realised all Europe's post-war dreams of eggs, fruit and milk in a peaceful America. The man who ran it was Hispanic, but from way back: his daughter couldn't take in that there could be countries like mine where you bought limes singly; they crushed a cartonfull daily, and it flowed from a tap. Rich. Ricos.

Lime juice; raisins; chilli-powdered beef jerky. Nights I wasn't hungry. Most nights I walked back from the mid-city bus stops late, sometimes almost all the way back from the Wah Wah Sing and Gutierrez Mortuary at the end of Sunset; walking fast but calmly, hat on and clutched against the warm off-building gusts, never through the lots, the cop cars already shrieking. Nights I was tired. My eyes were sore with street grit and dazzle off the pool in the garden at the Getty. Or I'd walked up a canyon, Laurel say, where the traffic had not met a solo pedestrian before and whumped by in waves, hurling out empty cans. Or lingered all afternoon at the Gene Autrey museum listening to a reading of the journal of an overland immigrant in an epidemic moment – not knowing, she wrote, if 'the high side boards of the wagons might not be our coffins tomorrow'. Upstairs in the dream galleries, Yakima Canutt – filmed in old age among his rodeo trophies – explained his stunts. One Sunday I walked seventeen miles to Santa Monica for a first look at the Bay, bussed home, flossed the teeth by eating the jerky, fell asleep in my clothes.

The television was on but the sound low. The kids a few doors along had the Shopping Channel on loud. The screen had shown the dramatised weather – a young woman with big hair describing the haze, and its burning-off, as if it were her audition piece. Reception and colour patchy.

I was patchy. The morning I flew there I left a letter for a man of whom I had held hopes for a year. The letter made desire explicit; asked for an end to ambiguity; promised to take a no to the jaw like a pro. He was a movie fan, downstairs in the front rows in the local Odeon or Gaumont, for 40 years. Almost everything I came across was shipped back to him. Like sourdough toast in The Pantry, and the clear-eyed no-longer young man on the next stool to me: 'How's the steak, Dave, worth the drive?' said the counterman. Dave had been on the road for two hours coming back from location for a steak. He'd been a farmer, he said, till his back went. Then a stunt driver, twenty years. It got easy when there was a Jacuzzi in a truck out on site, you pulled your tricks relaxed and flexed. The thick white diner showed as the steak diminished, but he couldn't quite finish it. Trashing new cars, he said, nothing better: get into a new car, close the windows, savour 'that bitchen new car smell', light a cigarette and let it burn down to scar the dashboard. 'I had one this show, three miles on the clock. Only three miles. And I totalled it.'

That would travel the Atlantic. Also Dietrich's gold-dusted, almost ginger wig, from the old Max Factor HQ, and the photographs on its wall of Max's first shop in Hill Street. Mrs Max and the hired help were wig-making – postiches and transformations and toupées in the old sense, complex false structures for women. (All that would be here was implicit in those re-presentations of desirability. Heads of hair were bought, for cash, in village Europe.) The movies, a name for people not pictures, would just have arrived at this rail-head town, where wildflowers grew either side of the tracks. Mrs Max knotted dyed peasant hair on a mesh base, and the sons stirred the liquid whitening vats: it was any immigrant's basic business. A bakery. A grocery.

I wanted to offer the man in his London attic a present from his dream America, and I couldn't afford The Searchers scenario in its clear sealed bag from the memorabilia shop on Hollywood Boulevard. But under the remains of an arcade at Venice Beach was a store selling old clothes, machine washed into a sanitary limpness, and I had bought a patchwork quilt for him. I could pretend it cost no more than the 50-buck note he gave me, left over from his own tentative trip. Other quilts piled at the back were silk crazies, or expensive because they had been made by the stricter sects, but this quilt was a weathered old glory flag, faded burgundy and ivory, indigo diagonals. To the sales-girls, 60s minifrocks were mythic, beyond historic. But quilts of the Twentieth Century were a local commonplace, goods bought in yard sales when the house was cleared by death. We folded and curled it up tightly, a blanket roll for that pale sand outside – that was cold to sit on before the sun broke through.

Grains fell from the quilt when I spread it across my bed. Several machine-tumblings for cleanliness had partially pulled it apart. Most of the thread ties, each of six strands of cotton (in that quiet green of kitchen paintwork 70 years ago) were unknotted, but they were sewn right through, and none were missing. The stitching of the patches was going, sand grains had seeped inside through the gaps. I lay on the bed by the light of the TV, waiting for the movie *Hondo* to begin. It was cold and I wrapped the quilt over me during the film, re-tieing the green threads in reef knots with my eyes on the screen.

Nightly for the next week, the quilt was neatly laid over the back of the one chair in the room when I got home, late. I'd been to the movies, for the picture palaces rather than the footage, coming out warmed by the red lanterns of Grauman's, hazed with the glow of the newly wired-up El Capitan. Film houses, like the shops there, were only barns: four walls bare externally, inside mostly holding electric light. (Their goods looked no good isolated under the flat sun.) The buses back from Westwood, from along Wilshire Boulevard, were cold, and tenser after dark, despite the polite and stoic drivers. On almost every bus, the same poem in Spanish, something like: 'Don't go for the man who wants you, he'll say and do anything. Look instead for the man who has given up on desires.'

Another night, one of the bar's temporary regulars (regular regulars were firemen, narcs cops, partying secretaries) took me to see his job. Brad, the lighting man out of Las Vegas, second generation – his father had made the hitching thumb sign. D'ya ever see somebody blow those tubes, he said, as I drew on the napkin the fantastic lettering of the Stardust sign. I hadn't thought of their creation, not even in the LA Museum of Neon, looking up at the old Kinema signs that might briefly be press-buttoned into life. Blown glass tube is naturally baroque – you never saw it used for Roman letters. Brad named the colours: magenta, hot pink, pool blue. He wasn't neoning, though. He was fixing the old Myron Ballroom a few hundred yards down the road as the new Shark Club, a spin-off of the Vegas place. Ya don't know it? Oldest dance-hall in town, several thousand could circulate on its sprung wood floors. Then Miz Myron bought it in 1945, 46, ran it through jive and jitterbug and black GIs and rock 'n roll, and she was still the owner, still a sharpie, 84 or that might be 86. When he put in his estimates for lighting the lots around she queried whether he needed round or square cable. Not to be bilked.

He was an enthusiast, he walked me down to the Ballroom. On its middle layer they'd almost finished the disco. The sound waves there would have physical force, would toss the girls' hair like wind. The young workers were sitting on carpets slutty with food cartons, and treated Brad as an old dullard. At his request one switched on a laser that turned a chandelier to rubies and blood drops, or at least Max's Blondeen lipstick, and the arrhythmic flashes of the strobe lighthoused far out of the crush doors, open for an evening wind. Brad and the chief rigger bivouacked on cots in W C Fields's dressing room, deep in sweaty basements barricaded by chairs. Absolutely the pits. We clambered up into the loft. Three filth-clarted witchballs still hung there, a gone magic among the Kliegls; and you could see the original wall and roof ribs, they looked to be about 1911 or so, studded with the sockets for the first excitement of electric bulbs. A box of darkness put up to be lit. Brad wanted to shine pearly white across the lots around, which would make girls feel safe as they parked their cars for a night at the Shark.

We walked across to the old Mayan Cinema. In the yellow darkness between two street lamps, it was a lump. He had a proposal to reclaim its sandstone facade. First, he would shoot out those sodium horrors on the pavement. Then, he would restore savagery to the shallow bas-reliefs copied from temples – with ambers to deepen shadows, pink-white mobilising the bones of the flat faces. And tiny brilliant beams to awaken the eyes. Roberto Salvatore at Max Factor described the making-up of a movie face just so, and recited colours too: sallow, Spanish, Mexican, Arab or Hindu, Mulatto, Mikado, Lavender, and Light and Dark Negro.

Brad wanted to drive me to Las Vegas to meet his father and see the Strip signs. To him, LA was fertile city. Wet. The multi-colour light of a city rises, he said, until it makes one beam of whiteness that pierces to the ionosphere.

My room seemed warmer. The maid, who had spoken once, to ask if my hat was from Michoacan, which it was, had laid the folded quilt on the end of the bed. Every floor of 444 was alight.

I picked over the quilt in daylight. (The salt haze reached even there, cold: I lay in. The coffee shop was open again. I think the baby was christened José.) Most of the materials must have been around 1930. Its backing was coarse flowery calico, strips machined together, texture so crude that they might have been the flour or feedgrain sacks merchants had printed decoratively so farmers' wives would favour their firm for the cloth. But the pieces seemed too large even for opened-up sacks. The main fabric of the right side was a cotton print that felt mealy and cheap, yet had a far higher warp count than the back. The patches were mostly a dull rose or blue, from a limited supply of ill-matched cloths. Some sombre Sunday-meeting textiles, cream stars or spots on dark backgrounds. A rough shirting, washed thin but still too heavy, and stockinette, meant for underwear, its knit construction distorted by use. A few square inches of a far older voile, so fine that most of the weft had worn away: one such patch had been crudely re-covered with a paisley, the kind of material used in the 40s for wrap-over pinafores. There were tiny fragments of cottons, a yellow one, unique and so small that it must have been a mail-order sample clipping.

I bought a second quilt for myself a few days later in Venice Beach, a skilled piecing of Art Deco lawns and ginghams, not tied but quilted in a frame. The curves of the stitching rippled through the squares. It was spare but its makers had enough yardage, all of it unworn: there was cash, and a store in town, and girls young enough to have pretty frocks they out-grew.

This quilt's patches had a different narrative. All but the samples had been recovered from exhausted clothes. That shirting, that voile was pre-1920. Before marriage, or at its start? She must have been without company: on a farm? She had nobody to exchange pieces with, and the sewing was all by one hand except that cobbled-on forties job. No sociable frame.

It would have to be mended and strengthened before it was given to him.

The Hollywood Boulevard Woolworth's had a plastic-bubbled sewing kit, but the threads were synthetic and the needles rusty. That salt haze penetrated. The telephone book listed an embroidery shop just past the Beverly Wilshire hotel, so I walked down there, in the now-familiar long curve ambling through the western oases, on ribbons of sidewalk, sprinklered cool, the pressured mist rising past the ankle. Green shade all the way, or violet over half the court of a low Spanish apartment block. Most of the dogs that threw themselves at fences or gates, barking, were twice human bodyweight, but the fences were distant, across the lawns. Between dogs were five and ten minute lengths of birdsong. Some orioles. There was no other company. I used to carry a small shoulder bag, and the security firm cars badged with liveries would slow to pace with me, surveilling. Once I was bagless, they drove past.

Off Wilshire, the English saleswoman had cotton thread, even had the kind of size ten German needles I like, so fine both ends will prick. On a bed of curlicued iron wire upstairs in the Ralph Lauren shop on Rodeo Drive there was a comforter in the same Old Glory colours as the quilt, but it was a certified antique and cost over $2000. Its makers must not have been desperate for warmth. It was almost unwadded.

The panhandler on the bus back had a clever line, worth more than the two bucks I gave him. He flattered his marks they were too good-looking not to have cars. (I don't drive.) The dollars were loose in my pocket, drawn $100 at a time from the bank nearest the Wells Fargo museum − an excuse to call in to look at the black lacquered safes with Japanesey paintings, at the company telegraph code book which reduced whole sentences for those in transit to a few near-nonsense words. (For instance, Kroog, very low; Krore, be prepared for the worst; Kubus, will not recover; Knug, died last night, and Kirat, arrange to ship the body home.) A bundle of a hundred clean bills was too thick to carry in my pocket. Twenty would do. I could feed to bursting for days on that, and the coin change paid for transport. The girls at the Venice Beach rags store thought their sister homewares shop up Topanga Canyon might know more about their sources of quilts, so I walked up from the Pacific Highway. Two black hawks patrolling high over the wildflowers, hot colours only, no blues. Smells of Sunday dinner from the sagebrush. Two wan blonde girls reading the stapled-up notices by the health food store: 'These cats have a protective grey coloring which prevents them from being seen by owls and coyotes.' 'Vegi-Match: We will computer match you with three other vegetarian singles for $25.'

The homewares proprietor was in his element, floating in the settlement's 1970 suspension. Where was the stock from? Well, maybe, some of it, it might come from yard sales in Valley towns. Closer than that she couldn't go. She was animated only when she wrongly thought she could sell me a silk throw over a century old. It was amateur, a rich girl's amusement, never used, no abrading even on the untwisted floss of the satin-stitched flowers. She had no idea of its past. It didn't look as if it was from this city, unless it came out by train in the founding years of the Atcheson, Topeka and the Santa Fe railroad. I couldn't imagine the red plush whorehouse girls labouring on this between tricks. And the piece was too early to be the time-killing project of some retiree's wife from the Middle West, shaded from the sun behind holland blinds. Did a lodging-house keeper, a woman – getting by in the state of the new canned fruits – stitch this as parlour work?

Rules of behaviour don't translate. Randolph the lawyer and manicured Johnnie, veteran of the race-tracks, wouldn't understand why I couldn't accept the offer of beer, or only accepted after I'd bought them a round first. Refusing meant I could get two beers relaxed with them, and say yes to going on to Mak's Bar for a third. They drove, two cars, though it was only minutes away on foot. The Vietnamese waitress was 20 years older than her girlish fall of black hair, her skittishness. Randolph biographed everyone: she was putting her son and daughter through USC. A customer to whom she said 'spe-she-all' often and deferentially was Japanese, a *nisei* grown up to be a judge. We moved on for a last drink at the Tender Trap at Sixth and Alvarado – where, said Randy, none of us should be. Though I'd walked through there, too. I was trying to remember the mouth diagrams which are Korean Hangul syllables on the shop signs – enjoying the pavement crowding and the way you bought any drink, even ginseng tea, by the generosity of a quart cup.

To salvage those quilt patches of voile where the warp threads only were left, I had to tramline –°which is to re-invent the weft with parallel rows of stitches. They were secured into the sheet of calico, bleached by use, which backed the pieces. One morning, sleepless at four, I unpicked the ends of the quilt, sealed like an envelope by a crude line of machining. Inside, not shop-bought cotton wadding, but an old, worn-thin counterpane of a striped hand-weave in sand and dirt colours. Initials RL, roughly stitched, hardly call it embroidery, on the border. The maid draped the chair with the finer quilt, but spread that one over the bed each morning, carefully, never dislodging the needle, never loosening work in progress. She wouldn't tell me her name. Her black plait of hair bounced off her spine as she worked.

    I'd been tramping the sea-coast highway for days trying to keep on the beach and off the roadside. The first few body shocks from the air displaced by trucks of sixteen wheels almost exhilarated, then physical fearfulness set in. It was slow going through sand, unless on the water-firmed margin along the tideline. We were outside the bathing season, and the beaches were unpeopled all week, except for a few hard boys, suited-up on their boards off Dan Blocker. When I came out of the beach washroom at Zuma, turning towards the road, a police-car stopped, waited for me to catch up. Window down. Empty vista. Heads out. You know a woman got murdered in there? Killed for her red foreign car by a couple boys out of New Mexico? (Were they being courteous or trying to induce nervousness?)

    'Nobody gets into my house without they call me first,' said the girlish woman in the bar at Trancas. 'I have a quarter taped to the front door with a note, says take the quarter and call me if you want to see me. Unless the canyon's on fire, don't knock.' She was talking to the hostess. Another old girl entered, with long hair past her shoulders, escorted by a meaty man. She'd been east to be hypnotised out of smoking, cleaning her lungs for her fiftieth birthday. I kept fingering the packet of new needles in my pocket. We went to Point Dume, a melancholy settlement, its salt-resistant foliage dark, the sun setting through it. I knew some wistful zones – the concrete villas, say, behind the cemetery in the Budapest hills early in a winter's morning – but this was sadder. They'd lived here twenty years. He acted. Second villain on *Magnum*. Saw you repeated yesterday, said the barman. At the stop, a grave old gentleman asked in Spanish if I would put out my hand to flag down the bus. It will stop for you, he said. Second in the queue was a film-maker from Mexico City: talking, talking, in English, of the proposal he dreamt of making to Cher for a special. He imagined her as a stream of Bob Mackie diamante, and the hair, the cherry hair.

What I thought of as I restored the quilt, as the light came up one morning, was this. On Santa Monica Pier, a long horizontal photograph, framed, of California beauty queens, near the boardwalk in the first years of the abbreviation of bathing costumes. Their faces, their bodies were within the stencils of their period, their brows were monumental, their legs not elongated. They had dry curls. But perhaps every tenth female in the line registered as modern, since the soft, tight, black of their mono-garments was near enough to what was strutting the boulevards. Those tenth ones couldn't be disregarded as safely defused by time.

In the carousel pavilion at the pier's end was a flicker book machine – a quarter a go. Chaplin, of course. But I kept seeing behind him the long-gone sunlight on a wooden wall.

The old patch of seamstress's skin on the second joint of my index finger had hardened again with driving the needle.

Brad was sullen in Hanks, complaining audibly to his rigger of my neglect. My good-talking company was a Hispanic law student on his way to Barcelona. A laundry delivery-man remembered his native Watts as the towers went up: no, too fast a verb, we agree on accreted. And there was Randolph. Nothing was explicable to Randolph. Not the walking on the tide-line, not the pleasures of the buses. What was the best time I had? The Saturday at Our Lady of The Angels, when there was a first communion feria. That court between church and its offices, black and white with tux'ed little grooms and veiled bridelets thwacking each other with ribboned candles. There were stalls of melon and pineapple slashed open, ices. The midriffs of the mothers had happy fat, the first generation of surplus. Some grandmothers in black seemed even to have replumped under their wrinkled skins. And the exuberance. 'Like the Chico stuff?' asked Randolph. I can remember how the first surplus tasted, the first excess sweetness, the beginnings of hope – through the bananas and

Whitsunday white nylon dresses – that we would not have to follow the narrative of our families. Time since was never so rich.

At Mak's bar, Randolph wanted to dance to Andrew Lloyd Webber on the juke, wanted to buy me dinner, at least in The Pantry. No. Despite his glamour, despite his Angeleno pronunciation (that worldwide-broadcast local dialect of sexual attraction). I'd almost completed the full length of the coast. There were only a few nights more when I'd make it back to my room to sew up the quilt's ends.

There was a possible history for the quilt. Guesswork. It didn't feel Californian, no matter how poor the Valley towns in the Depression. It seemed farm, lonely farm, mid-West farm; an urgent necessity for coverings gussied up, just, with what little could be reclaimed within one building. It could be (was that merely should be?) Okie. The comforter on the journey out there, hard-worn before, and then in, this state. That patch from the 40s nagged. The quilt was repatched only the once, about a decade after it was made, when the first of those frail voile pieces went — only tufts remained beneath. But the substitute was roughly cut, folded, sewn. If the same hand that made it, had also stitched that on, she had changed. Her patience had gone, or her tendons. The quilt had still been needed. That was a running repair.

Randolph stopped his silvery Jaguar on Figueroa, made an offer. His warmth would have been welcome to ameliorate the dryness. Yet the coast – no, the quilt – was the imperative. It had to go to the movie fan with strength restored to it, a chance of surviving into his future: he had said, again and again, his middle-aged move would be, green-carded, to America. That was his final new-start dream. And I wanted him to take the quilt once more west, optimistically.

The size of the steaks.

On that last stretch of walking from car door to room, the sidewalk derelict sat up from under his blanket right at my ankle, and yelled soundlessly.

The quilt was out full, over the bed, over me, needle in hand, about five foot more of ladder-stitching. *The Shootist* on the television: 444 half-lit. The telephone rang. Randolph was in the lobby, ignoring the disapproval of the Sikh proprietors.

He hadn't taken a negative for an answer.

Folded and rolled again by the maid, still refusing her name; roped and tied with Woolworth's bandannas from the branch on Broadway;

boxed for security by Panam, which had them sniffed, the quilts went east. Mine lay in a chest, unused, until I gave it to a pregnant friend, shivering with fear despite summer. 'I have slept under the quilt almost every night since you gave it to me,' she wrote later, 'it usually travels with me – and I regard it as having magical healing powers.' Her son (the baby was a boy; he was christened Samuel) felt the same way. The movie fan did not reply to the letter, but after a month and over a beer, he said no, not interested. His sole attempt to get a green card was to send his name to the pan-European lottery. Although he was a Liverpudlian, almost Irish, he was not lucky. When he married the perfect woman some years later, she found the quilt in his cupboard, loved it, threw it over their sofa. She took him to live in America.

Veronica Horwell works for the *Guardian*, and is an expert on clothes.

Alfred Corn

Behind

> *Vade retro, Satanas*

'Innocent', in need of a good scratch, as Auden once
Wrote about a horse's. And, since neither animals
Nor poems are alien to humans, then the flesh cushion
We sit on must feel both innocence and itch alike.
Symmetrically bisected, hard for us to see

Till helped by mirrors we often wish had not, the thing's
Never bared but to our docs and dearests – proof
That *real* love is based on complete, near-medical knowledge.
The body's portals also recall one of Jesus'
Rare wisecracks, how we're defiled not by what goes in us,

No, but what comes out, a truth eroded lately
By Golden Arches speedfeed. McNugget, anyone?
Meanwhile, all who've been the butt of practical jokes,
Will sympathise with the body's namesake counterpart,
Victim of childhood spankings, kicks both figurative

And literal, a cringing target for hypodermics.
Buonarotti's *David* and the *Rokeby Venus* taught us
Its beauty, and even our cold, high-tech age considers
The 'booty' an erotic Eden, sourcing similes
So apt they are already trite, like 'melon' and 'bubble'.

Though champion weightlifters will squat and heft two-fifty
To pump their glutes heroic, some people (and some peoples)
Are *born* endowed, incarnating the stylish S
Shape of the dancer and prehistoric petroglyph.
Slangsmiths joined the corps by conflating British 'arse'

With a standard beast of burden (*O Bottom, thou art changed!*)
And then suffixing 'hole', to coin an epithet
Even hotheads who've hardly seen one daily fall back on —
Which suggests, when you ponder the figure's vehicle,
That slurs may enshrine love-hate relations. I mean, could they

Or Swift's own Celia ever do without one? No way.
Oh, and my kind deserves a nod, explorers bent
On pleasure, blazing a trail now well traveled by both
Orientations, anatomists who solved the Riddle
Of the Sphincter — and made a lively entrance of their exits.

Alfred Corn has published nine books of poetry in the US, a novel and a collection of essays. He has been living in London this year, teaching for the Poetry School and the Arvon Foundation. This summer he will be directing a poetry writing course at Wroxton College in Oxfordshire.

Our Bold

Cod Piece

In 2001, the Royal Court theatre mounted a production of *Fucking Games* by Grae Cleugh. It was directed by Dominic Cooke and was memorable for two things. There was at least one anal rape staged. And one of the gay characters represented the tiny misogynist faction of gay consciousness and referred to women as 'fish'. It must be some similar – anachronistic – prejudice that skewed Hilton Als's indignant reading of Wilde's *The Importance of Being Earnest* (*New Yorker* 8 May 2006). He was 'troubled' by 'the more sobering dialogue'. Brace yourselves.

'When Gwendolen meets young Cecily in the country, she engages her in some particularly sly exchanges:

GWENDOLEN: Cecily, Mamma, whose views on education are remarkably strict, has brought me up to be extremely short-sighted; it is part of her system; so do you mind my looking at you through my glasses?
CECILY: Oh! Not at all, Gwendolen. I am very fond of being looked at.

[Sinister stuff, you'll agree}

Or:

CECILY: This is no time for wearing the shallow mask of manners. When I see a spade, I call it a spade.

GWENDOLEN: (*sarcastically*) I am glad to say that I have never seen a spade. It is obvious that our social spheres have been widely different.

This kind of nastiness takes something away from the high finish of Wilde's presentation, by making one of his personal failings all too clear: his distaste for women. Wilde's female characters always address the most cutting lines to one another, while the men bumble on. Gwendolen's cattiness (like Lady Bracknell's) feels real because it sounds like Wilde talking. The women are his mask.'

Andrew McNeillie

Two Poems

Chanson D'Hiver

I lie awake for more than half the night,
like a northern summer, my mind suffused
with light, though it's deep winter still
and long days are a dream that's yet to come
when short nights keep a bonfire never quite
gone out. I call this hope, if you will.

An oyster-catcher on a roof-ridge pipes
night ashore and day aboard in light
like wreaths of smoke; and, even from this far,
I can hear the tide crunch packed air,
quarrying the bay for white sand
What is it that I cannot say, to you?

It's not that I dislike the cold air:
rain turned to sleet and flakes no longer hesitant
blinding the headland with light,
like a poke in the eye with a sprung twig,

and metaphor stranded for the duration
out in the wilderness of frozen pipes.

The world as it is I can take if it exists,
as appearances, and commonsense, insist.
But they always insist too much, the facts
and certainties their own undoing,
for life is all becoming, and this winter night
I lie here wide awake because of you.

February Song

It was a false evening
very like a dawn.
I heard a song-thrush singing
from an empty thorn.

Something in the light
encouraged it to sing
and as it sang so I have sung
and been as wrong.

Andrew McNeillie is the Literature Editor at Oxford University Press. He is the author of two books of poetry: *Nevermore* (2000) and *Now, Then* (2002).

Ian McEwan

Flies

The following scenes are taken from Ian McEwan's sequel to David Cronenberg's 1986 film The Fly.

The Geena Davis character, Veronica Quaife (here Ronnie), ended that movie pregnant by Seth Brundle (Jeff Goldblum). Here, Ronnie's worst fears prove to be correct – and her twin sons Tim and Charlie gradually begin their biological morph into flies. We join the script at this point – where Tim is already in advance of Charlie who is using his nascent insect brilliance to solve the problem. In the background, there is corporate villainy exerting external pressure on the family.

The film was unmade.

INT. BARN DAY.

The barn is enormous. Undivided areas are used by the family for sleeping and cooking. There is a 'living room' comprising old car seats. CHARLIE is in the workshop area. Trestle tables are loaded with computer equipment and electronics gear. Power cables drop down from the rafters.

As RONNIE enters, CHARLIE lets out a penetrating whoop. RONNIE'S expression relaxes when she realises that CHARLIE is not distressed, he's exultant. He's very speedy, his mind is power-driven. The tell-tale signs. He barely registers the puppy which RONNIE sets on the ground.

CHARLIE

I'm into the programme, Mom! I know how it works and it's a piece of pure genius 'cos it reads the whole DNA sequence of any living creature then it digitalises the codons and then you send it by radio and at the same time on another channel you convert the tissue into an electron stream – and POW! – you decode and assemble it at the other end, you can zap a whole human being from one place to another at the speed of light. Beam me up!

As CHARLIE is ranting on, RONNIE comes towards him slowly, anxiety gathering in her expression. She reaches him.

RONNIE

That's great news, Charlie. You're a genius. But you're speedy. Turn round...

She lifts his t-shirt and examines his back. There on the shoulder blades are the purplish areas of ruptured skin where the wings are beginning to grow. He turns back to look at her and catches her mood. His voice drops.

CHARLIE

Mom, is it starting? Is that why I'm feeling like...

RONNIE draws CHARLIE to her.

It's going to happen to me, isn't it? I'm going to look like Tim. ... I think I'd rather be dead...

Close on CHARLIE as RONNIE enfolds him.

RONNIE

Shush now... We're going to carry on with this work...

CHARLIE
Mom... Have you seen what's happening to Tim's eyes? ...I'm really frightened...

RONNIE
... we're going to build this machine and beat this thing. You believe in me don't you, Charlie?

CHARLIE nods. RONNIE kisses his head.

So, we've got to move fast. You can run the program ...

CHARLIE
Yeah, but...

RONNIE
And I can digitalise the DNA.

CHARLIE
Listen, you need a whole lot of...

RONNIE
No, you listen. You're going to write me a computer shopping list OK? Right now.

CHARLIE
But Mom, we need a supercomputer, we're gonna have to download a whole person, a whole genome onto a chip. ..

RONNIE
I know. Leave that to me. Where's Tim?

As CHARLIE turns back to his computer screen, he nods up at the rafters.

RONNIE *takes a flashlight and strides into the centre of the barn.*

Tim?

We follow the flashlight beam as it probes the dark recesses of the enormous timbered roof. We see something move, then it is gone.

Tim!

RONNIE *takes something from her pocket.*

Want to see what I've got here?

Another glimpse of movement. Some dirt is dislodged from a rafter and falls to the floor. Then the beam picks out TIM'S *form moving rapidly along – upside down and under a beam. He reaches the wall and seems to half crawl, half bound down it, head first.*

What arrives in front of us is still recognisably a boy, but the transformation to fly has advanced hugely. He is naked to the waist to allow space for the wing cases on his back which are now almost a foot long. His body is twisted and stooped forwards, there are thick black hairs growing on his limbs, and above the line of his cheekbones are little growths that foreshadow compound eyes. His face is beginning to lose its familiar outlines as human skin and insect chitin merge into a flakey mess.

The puppy takes one look at TIM *and runs for cover.*

Then, on RONNIE. *She is doing her best to treat* TIM *as though he were simply ill. She fights against her disgust, and her impulse to regard him as an alien. She needs to stay in touch with the child she knows is in there.*

However bizarre, the scene that follows also has an everyday, domestic quality.

TIM'S *voice is slow, but still his own.*

TIM
Charlie ate all my candy bars. I left them under the bed...

CHARLIE

Mom... It isn't true.

RONNIE
Look what I found for you, Tim.

She offers TIM a Rubik Cube puzzle. He seizes it eagerly and begins solving it.

TIM
Oh yeah. I like these. But they're so easy... Mom, I marked my candy and put it in a special place...

RONNIE
OK, OK...

Close on CHARLIE who has followed RONNIE into the centre of the barn. This is his own future he is witnessing.

CHARLIE
Tim, that was yesterday. And you ate them.

RONNIE speaks gently.

RONNIE
It's OK. I've got some more.

TIM, stretching out a deformed, partly crumbling hand trying to take the chocolate bar.

Uhuh. What do you say?

TIM
Please Mom... please Mom... please ...

A spurt of yellowish viscous fluid leaves TIM'S mouth and splats to the floor.

RONNIE averts her eyes and fights her disgust. Close on CHARLIE'S look of horror.

CHARLIE
Oh no... No...

RONNIE
Now Tim. I want you to promise to take this outside before you eat it.

TIM
Yeah, yeah, promise. I promise.

As TIM takes the candy his body goes into a spasm of anticipation. It's all his human mind can do to overcome his fly nature which has no time for promises.

The viscous digestive fluid drips on to the bar and begins to dissolve it.

RONNIE
Out! I said out. Take it in the yard.

She shoos him towards the door. Then she turns to CHARLIE.

To work, Charlie. I'm driving to town after lunch. I've got my list. You've got four hours to write yours.

EXT. ROAD ON THE EDGE OF TOWN. DAY.

The town serves a large military base. Various businesses and civilian research outfits have grown up around it. Many of them are spread out along this road.

RONNIE slows down the pick-up and cruises by lots selling ex-military vehicles, hippy psychic software companies, virtual reality workshops, oceanographic research, a skateboard research and design centre, a wilderness survival store – a whole underworld of unofficial expertise.

She turns into an open gate where a sign reads Scientific Materials and Instruments Track-down Service. She drives on in.

EXT. SMITS LOT.   DAY

RONNIE gets out of the pick-up. In her hand, sheets of computer print-out.

Silence. She walks down an avenue of fascinating junk – submarine and helicopter parts, a pottery kiln, cranes and hoists, mining equipment etc – towards a large wooden cabin, the SMITS sales office.

By the porch a chained alsatian growls. But RONNIE pushes past it and enters.

INT. SMITS SALES ROOM.   DAY.

The place is in low light, and crammed ceiling-high with scientific equipment of every conceivable kind.

Watching her suspiciously from behind a counter is the sales assistant, BOB – an overweight slob. His manner is faintly contemptuous. From a back room behind him, the sound of a TV.

BOB
Hey now. Dr Quaife.

RONNIE
Oh, hi. I need more stuff. Did you find the computer?

BOB
Pete!

PETE, the SMITS owner emerges from the back room, scratching his belly and yawning.

PETE

Oh hi. We located a Kray. A gigabyte of RAM, TL operating system. You know how to run that, Dr Quaife?

RONNIE

Can you get the other stuff?

PETE and BOB glance at the list and look at each other. They can't take her seriously.

PETE

Well now... iridium alloy. I get it. You're uh building a spaceship right...

The door opens. Another customer. RONNIE has her back to the door.

BOB

Be right with you...

PETE tosses the sheet down on the counter.

PETE

Someone put you up to this?

RONNIE

Do you want the business or not? If you don't –

PETE

Like how are you proposing to cut the iridium. With scissors?

BOB

Yeah. From your sewing box...

GUNTHER
We'll be using an arc vector cutter. Put it on the list.

RONNIE turns, astonished.

RONNIE
Gunther!

PETE
You guys are together?

RONNIE and GUNTHER exchange a look. GUNTHER, wearing faded jeans and hiking boots has a back pack slung over his shoulder. He's dusty from long hard travelling. He shrugs. RONNIE hesitates, then smiles uneasily.

RONNIE
Yeah... I guess.

INT. PICK-UP TRUCK. DAY.

RONNIE drives fast down a dirt track – Route 84 – along a cliff top.

GUNTHER
It was simple enough. I figured you'd be in the market for a supercomputer. So I watched the notice boards on the 'net...

RONNIE tenses. Instinctively she glances in the mirror. There's a car.

RONNIE
...Those guys in the store put it out on the internet?

GUNTHER
How else...

RONNIE
That means Quantz can find me too...

RONNIE brings the pick-up to a sharp halt by the side of the track. She watches the car go by.

EXT. Rt 84. CLIFF TOP.   DAY

RONNIE crosses the track and is standing on the cliff edge, looking out to sea, struggling with the turmoil of her thoughts. GUNTHER comes beside her. A beat, then –

GUNTHER
Ronnie. I know you'd rather I wasn't here but there's something...

She turns to him

RONNIE
Look, Gunther. What's happening now... I've been waiting for it all their lives. Always looking for the first sign, and never knowing how it's going to come. Something in their behaviour, the foods they like, some little thick black hair that I'll see when I'm bathing them... Now it's here, and it's frightening, it's miserable. But the worst of it is the humiliation. Seeing Tim's dignity going, the way they're losing their childishness, what's human... being eaten away... and replaced... It's humiliating, for them, for me. That's why I don't want anyone around. That's why I've never let another person in on this.

GUNTHER waits. RONNIE takes a breath and sighs.

I fight for them, and I'll go on fighting for them. You're looking at a fighting machine. And it's made me hard... Keeping someone like you away... The boys love you... You've been very kind.. And sometimes I feel completely alone, just one more helpless parent up against an incurable genetic disease...

A beat. They hold each other's gaze.
She looks away.

GUNTHER

Being hard isn't the same as being strong. I'd like you to let me in. I want to help. Besides, I've got nowhere else to go. Quantz tried to kill me, and I had to take the road. These are serious people.

RONNIE
Gunther... I'm sorry.

He takes her hand.

RONNIE
I am glad you're here... Really glad...

They continue to hold each other's gaze, and for a moment it seems they might kiss. But this is not the time.

When you meet Tim... Try not to show him... That you're... Remember, he's still a little boy...

GUNTHER nods. RONNIE sighs, and lets his hand drop.

Better get back to them...

EXT. Rt 84. COAST LANDSCAPE. DAY.

Drive-by. The dirt track, the cliffs, mountains and sea. A high angle (helicopter shot) establishes the loneliness and isolation of the place.

EXT. JAGO'S PLACE. DAY.

RONNIE *slows down as she passes* JAGO'S *place and waves to MR and MRS JAGO*

EXT. BARN. DAY.

She pulls the pick-up to a stop outside the barn and cuts the engine. RONNIE *and* GUNTHER *exchange a look. She's not looking forward to him seeing the boys.*
She gives his hand a squeeze.

RONNIE
Are you sure you're ready for this?

GUNTHER
Yeah. You ready to count me in?

She takes a deep breath and gets out of the pick-up.

INT. BARN.   DAY.

CHARLIE *is exactly where* RONNIE *left him – at the computer, in a pool of artificial light, typing and mousing at frenzied speed. Strewn around the floor at his feet and across the make-shift desk are dozens of candy bar wrappers.*
CHARLIE *glances round but he doesn't stop. On screen, an advanced math program. He's speeding. His intellectual energy is unrelenting.*
But when he sees GUNTHER *he leaps to his feet and throws himself into the man's arms.*

CHARLIE
Gunther!

GUNTHER
Charlie. How ya doing kid...

CHARLIE breaks away and, talking a double speed, leads GUNTHER by the hand to the computer.

CHARLIE
How d'you get here? It's great 'cos we badly need a biologist. I mean, we're gonna need to know a whole lot about expressing cell polarity and the gradients of positional information, you know, like, if certain genes establish lineage boundaries which register gradients of positional information...

RONNIE comes and places her hands soothingly on CHARLIE'S shoulders.

RONNIE
Charlie. Charlie. Slow down. You're way out of your depth. Do the programming and leave the genetics to me. Now did you eat something?

CHARLIE
I'm into this, Mom. Gunther, take a look. There's an integral membrane protein encoded...

RONNIE
And where's Tim?

CHARLIE
He's round the back. He got hungry. See, Gunther...

RONNIE
Oh God.

She moves away to find TIM. GUNTHER puts his hand on CHARLIE'S shoulder before following her.

GUNTHER
Charlie. Take a calm look at the gene products that read polarity and express it.
You need a lesson in the basics.

EXT. BARN.   DAY

GUNTHER catches up with RONNIE as she hurries along the side of the barn towards the rear.

RONNIE
Maybe you shouldn't see this…

They round the corner. A scene of desolation. TIM has taken half a dozen plastic trash bags from the garbage cans and strewn their contents across the ground. He has been picking through the mess for rotten food. Now he's perched agilely on the rim of a garbage can lovingly dissolving and ingesting a decayed slice of pizza. Clouds of flies – fat, buzzing bluebottles – hover over the detritus. TIM presides over them.

Several rats have been drawn by the scent of the food. TIM'S eyes are bothering him. He keeps flicking and scratching at his cheekbone.

Close on GUNTHER. He understands genetics and he thought he was unshockable. But nothing could have prepared him for this – the spread of stinking, decaying food, the flies, the rats, and lording it over them all, the naked boy-insect, fluttering his nascent wings to maintain his balance on the rim of the garbage can.

RONNIE goes forward, GUNTHER hangs back. TIM does not see him at first.

RONNIE
Oh Tim!

RONNIE picks up a rock and hurls it. One of the rats retreats dragging by its jaws another far larger slice of pizza.

I left you plenty of food inside.

TIM cringes and looks ashamed.

TIM
I know... But it was all fresh... I'm sorry...

RONNIE throws another rock and approaches him.

RONNIE
Darling...

TIM
Mom, it's my eyes. They really hurt.

RONNIE
Try not to scratch them....

Watched by the amazed GUNTHER, RONNIE puts her arms around TIM. He cuddles up to her. He has become very dependent.

TIM
I don't want this. I want this to stop, Mom.
Why can't you make it stop?

RONNIE
Sssh now. Tim, I am going to make it stop. Now, let's get away from this garbage. Someone you know is here...

GUNTHER has been coming forward slowly, and as RONNIE turns TIM away from the garbage pile, the boy notices him. To be seen by someone other than his mother, someone TIM knows and likes, is a fresh humiliation.

Uh... Gunther... I didn't know...

TIM cannot bear to be seen. He tries to hide behind his mother. GUNTHER comes forwards, squelching through the putrescent mess until he is close enough to TIM to touch.

GUNTHER
Hey Cap'n...

TIM
What are you doing here?

GUNTHER
I've come to help you, pal.

TIM turns on RONNIE.

TIM
You said you wouldn't let anyone see me...

GUNTHER
She tried to stop me, but I pushed my way in, Cap'n.

TIM
Mom said she was going to make me better, and I'm getting worse.

TIM is moving away, deeply upset.

I know what I look like. I found a mirror.

TIM backs away towards the barn. He makes a sudden flying leap, landing on the side ot the barn. He shins up its vertical surface at speed. He crouches by the eaves looking down at RONNIE and GUNTHER.

TIM
Why don't you tell the truth? It's hopeless, and you know it. ..

RONNIE
Tim, please....

TIM
You ought to do what you did to my father. He was so far gone you had to finish him off like some kind of sick dog...

RONNIE
Tim. No!

TIM
But you won't...

RONNIE is distraught. She has forgotten GUNTHER'S presence.

RONNIE
Because I love you!

Her words have a startling effect. TIM is suddenly stilled, recalled to his childlike self. He is silent, looking down at her. Then he whispers

TIM
But you hate the sight of me.

He disappears through a gap in the roof, back into the safety of the dark roof space.
RONNIE stands among the garbage, staring after TIM.
GUNTHER stands by, uncertain what to say.

EXT. BARN. DUSK.

Long shot. Working in silence together, RONNIE and GUNTHER are shovelling the garbage into plastic sacks.

INT. BARN.   NIGHT.

RONNIE and GUNTHER sit in the dining area of the barn, at a makeshift table.

RONNIE has just served up some food. GUNTHER pours some wine. CHARLIE is still at the computer. The keys are rattling as furiously as ever.

There is no sign of TIM. After the conversation with him earlier, RONNIE is looking stressed. Her hand is shaking as she serves the food. GUNTHER registers this.

RONNIE
Charlie, give it a break. Come and eat.

CHARLIE
Can't... Anyway that food stinks!

RONNIE
Will you please get over here!

CHARLIE
Why don't you shout at Tim? He never comes to the table...

RONNIE
Charlie...

GUNTHER puts a restraining hand on RONNIE'S arm.

GUNTHER
I'll spend some time with him later...

RONNIE takes a deep breath. She takes a pull of her wine and stares at her food.

She can't eat it either. From high above them in the rafters, a stirring Pieces of debris are dislodged and drop to the floor. RONNIE meets GUNTHER'S eye. She cannot speak.

GUNTHER
Look.. uh. about Tim. These genes, these extra genes he has. You know how people talk of genes being selfish – meaning they're selected to shape our behaviour, to make us do whatever's necessary to get them into the next generation...

RONNIE
The selfish gene...

GUNTHER
Well, a better word might be ruthless.

She looks at him, waiting.

RONNIE
So?

GUNTHER
We don't have much time. Those fly genes have found a new home, and they're not going to give it up. It'll be a fight to the death, they'll make Tim fight us...

RONNIE
Yeah. We've got to move fast.

GUNTHER glances over in CHARLIE'S direction.

GUNTHER

We might have to concentrate on what's possible... There may be some difficult decisions...

RONNIE is immediately suspicious.

RONNIE

Like what? What are you saying?

GUNTHER backs off. It's too soon.

GUNTHER

Nothing... it's just, they're at different stages. Charlie'll co-operate, Tim's going to be something else... just preparing you...

RONNIE is angry. All the stress she feels suddenly finds a focus.

RONNIE

Preparing me for what. Come on. Say It.

GUNTHER

There's nothing more. I've just told you...

RONNIE'S voice rises. They are talking over each other.

RONNIE

If you've got something to say, say it!

GUNTHER

Ronnie, this is crazy...

RONNIE

Come on. What is this difficult decision?

What are you...

GUNTHER
You're getting me all wrong here...

RONNIE
Bullshit! What decision. What are you afraid of? That I can't take it? That I'm going to start crying? What do you think.

GUNTHER
Ronnie... listen Ronnie... you're over reacting. Take a deep breath and...

RONNIE
Deep breath!

CHARLIE has become aware of the row and has stopped working to watch and listen. Now, the old peacemaker in him asserts itself. He waits for his moment, then –

CHARLIE
Hey Gunther. I really need some help...

GUNTHER gratefully seizes the opportunity.

GUNTHER
Excuse me.

He goes over to CHARLIE. We stay on RONNIE.

Ok, Charlie. Let's take a look... You isolated the three genes?

She takes that deep breath, clasps her hands, lets her head drop. She's feeling crazy. She knows she's being tough on GUNTHER. But she also knows she cannot give up on TIM.

While GUNTHER'S and CHARLIE'S voices murmur on, she stands and crosses the barn and takes a long ladder which she rests against one of the high beams and begins to ascend.

These are their names right...

CHARLIE
Yeah, but I still don't understand how the gene products read polarity and express it...

GUNTHER
Wait wait. Take them one at a time. Here we are, here's a candidate, the gene we call frizzled which encodes membrane protein...

RONNIE reaches the top of the ladder. Her head and shoulders protrude into the dark, dusty roof space with its complicated struts and supports.

RONNIE
Tim?

We peer with her into the gloomy corners. Was that a movement? She whispers.

Tim, I want to talk to you... ..

Silence. Only the murmur of voices from below. We go closer on RONNIE.
She's desperate to re-establish contact with the boy after the afternoon's scene.

Tim?

Suddenly he appears from an unexpected direction. RONNIE starts. As well as her love, there is a growing element of fear which she tries to suppress.

Tim... I

TIM
You've got to send Gunther away. I don't want him here.

He edges closer. She finds herself backing away.

RONNIE
I need his help. I can't do all this by myself...

TIM
Why are you afraid of me?

RONNIE
Tim, I love you.

TIM
You don't. You hate everything about me. The way I eat, the way I look...

RONNIE
You're my darling boy, Tim...

TIM
I'm not a boy. You love Charlie and he's a boy. You don't want me...

Overcoming her fear, RONNIE stretches out a hand to him. There are tears in her eyes.

RONNIE
It isn't true. It isn't true. You're still my Timmy, you're still my boy and I love you just the same as I always did.

He begins to move away from her. He's starting to cry. It's a mournful piercing sound.

TIM

But I'm not a boy. Mommy... You can see... This is what I am. I want you to like me being this... I want you to love me like this... I'm not your boy...

TIM recedes into the gloom of the rafter space.
Close on RONNIE. She whispers.

RONNIE

Come back... Timmy, please come back....

This is confirmation of GUNTHER'S warning. The fact sinks in.

INT. BARN.   NIGHT.

Late at night. In the bedroom area of the barn. CHARLIE is asleep.
By the computer. RONNIE and GUNTHER work on into the night, keeping their voices low.
Then, a shift in angle. We are looking down on RONNIE and GUNTHER from high up, in the deep recesses of the rafters.
Then the reverse. Holding the puppy in his arms, TIM is watching the two below as they work towards removing his fly genes. On his face, an expression of deep mistrust. But there's something else on his face too. His eyes are leaking, seething, coagulating. There's a swelling at the top of his cheekbone. As we watch, something pushes up through the skin. A compound eye is beginning to form...

EXT/INT BARN.   DAY.

An explosive cut into a powerful hammer blow. GUNTHER is assembling the make-shift wooden frame for the pod.

Sunlight streams into the barn though huge doors which are open so that PETE and BOB from SMITS can bring in the super-computer. RONNIE is supervising the installation. CHARLIE is at her side.

Up in his usual place in the rafters, TIM, obscured in the gloom, watches the activity. His foot is giving him trouble. He crouches forward to rub it and a large piece of foot comes away in his hand. In its place is the hair covered sucker foot of a household fly.

TIM lets the half-decomposed portion of his foot drop to the floor. We follow it down. It lands in the centre of the barn unnoticed and is immediately trodden underfoot by PETE and BOB as they heave the equipment in.

Later. A printer is spewing out pages of blueprints from SETH BRUNDLE'S original plans. GUNTHER'S hand comes into shot and gathers the pages up. We follow him into the centre of the barn where the pod is now taking shape.

Later. RONNIE is setting up the new computer. GUNTHER is laying down power lines. Steel rack shelves have been erected for storing components.

CHARLIE is unpacking electronics parts and labelling and storing them on the shelves. He breaks off to try and reach a spot on his shoulder blade that is tormenting him.

INT. BARN. DAY.

Sudden silence. GUNTHER stands in the barn entrance surveying the scene. All around, the chaos of construction. Packing cases, tools, bits of equipment are everywhere. But there is a satisfying sense of completion – for the moment.

The pod is a wood and indium structure. It stands in the centre of the barn. Over by the wall, the super-computer is in place. Now the difficult work of marrying the hardware to the program can begin.

GUNTHER walks towards the pod and begins a casual inspection of the welding job on the indium alloy, and generally checking the structure.

A quick movement, a flitting shadow perhaps, makes him pause and turn and look.

But he seems to be alone in the barn. He resumes his inspection. As he comes round the side of the pod he hears a sound from the computing area. Again, he pauses – and there is nothing.

But now he's suspicious. He walks stealthily towards the bank of equipment which is piled well over six feet high. A gathering sense of threat.

As he walks round the banked equipment – a sudden shock as he comes upon TIM sitting at the console of the new computer.

Even in a day or two TIM'S metamorphosis had advanced noticeably. A compound and human eye are painfully merged, though it is clear that the human organ is losing out. The wings have advanced too, and stretch and flutter nervously, half folded against TIM'S body. His legs are now more fly than human, spindly, black and covered by thick black hairs.

With suckered hands TIM is typing and tilting his head to get a view of the computer screen through his compound eyes.

GUNTHER
Tim... What are you doing?

TIM turns slowly from the keyboard. Since we last saw him his mind has become fully resolved – he intends to remain a fly. His tone is deliberate.

TIM
You haven't asked me what I want..

As GUNTHER comes closer he realises that TIM is trying to erase the program.

GUNTHER
Hey... Wait... That's our separation program.

TIM
My father's work, Gunther. I know what he would have wanted me to do...

GUNTHER
Get away from there...

GUNTHER, overcomes his disgust and tries to push TIM away from the computer.

TIM springs to his feet and they go into a sickly clinch. TIM throws GUNTHER back, and turns again to the computer. GUNTHER recovers and grips TIM'S arm in one hand and tries to pull it clear.

They struggle. TIM releases a torrent of digestive fluids, most of which miss GUNTHER'S arm and go sizzling to the barn floor. But enough has touched him to burn through his shirt and cause him excruciating pain.

GUNTHER does the only thing he can think of – strike the creature hard in the face, just by the vulnerable mess of his eye.

At that moment, a shout from across the barn, and both man and boy-fly freeze.

RONNIE
Gunther!

RONNIE comes hurrying across, followed closely by CHARLIE.

With a child's cry of pain, TIM breaks free and staggers away, nursing his face.

He is no longer the frightening scheming monster. He makes the sounds of a normal sobbing child.

GUNTHER dashes to the kitchen area to rinse his arm at the tap. He shouts to RONNIE as she crosses the barn towards him.

GUNTHER
He was trying to erase the program...

Still crying, TIM scuttles quickly up the side of the barn.
As RONNIE brushes past she flashes at GUNTHER a scowl.

He was going to destroy all our work...

We move on with her. As she arrives at the foot of the ladder –

It would have been the end, for him and for Charlie.

RONNIE
Tim? Tim!

No reply. No sound.
RONNIE turns on GUNTHER.

RONNIE
Godammit. He's only a child!

RONNIE and GUNTHER hold each other's gaze angrily.

INT. QUANTZ CORPORATION. NIGHT.

NIPPLER hurries down a corridor.

INT. QUANTZ'S OFFICE.   NIGHT.

NIPPLER pushes his way in. QUANTZ is in conference with four EXECUTIVES. One empty sleeve of his suit jacket is tucked into a pocket.

NIPPLER
There's uh a development. We found her...

NIPPLER is constrained by the presence of the EXECUTIVES.

QUANTZ
Gentlemen. If you wouldn't mind. We'll pick it up tomorrow. First thing.

As the last EXECUTIVE is leaving, NIPPLER is reaching up to point to a large map of the USA.

NIPPLER

She's rented a place way out on an island just off the coast here. Hellstrom is with her. They've taken delivery of a Kray...

Even as he is speaking, QUANTZ is putting through a call.

QUANTZ

Larry? Yeah – I want the team. The whole team.

INT. BARN NIGHT.

RONNIE, half undressed, by CHARLIE'S bed, is making her nightly inspection of his back. The papery wings protrude a couple of inches now.
She kisses him.

RONNIE

It's going to be fine. Let's get some sleep.

GUNTHER in his own bed watches her longingly as she crosses to the wash basin.
Close on him.

EXT. FOREST NEAR BARN. NIGHT.

Long shot. High in a tree, at the end of a branch, a crouched figure perches silhouetted against the dawn sky.

INT. BARN.   NIGHT.

Half an hour later. The dawn light is greyish-blue. A prowling camera suggests a sleepless presence. It looks in on RONNIE, on GUNTHER. Then comes close and then closer, to CHARLIE.

He stirs in his sleep. He opens his eyes, and wonders what woke him.

A papery, rustling sound causes him to shift his gaze. A sudden shock. He scrambles up in bed.

Hunched at the foot of his bed is the figure of his brother, the boy-fly. It's a terrible sight in the semi-obscurity. The compound eyes are now fully formed.

The nose and mouth are beginning to shape themselves into a proboscis distorting the sound of his voice.

TIM
Charlie... Charlie.

CHARLIE
Oh no... Tim...

TIM
Listen... I came to tell you. It's going to be all right.

CHARLIE
I know. We're going to crack it. Mom says we –

TIM
No. You don't understand. You're going to be like me. You don't need to fight it. It's a beautiful thing... I want you to come with me.

CHARLIE
Oh no... No.

TIM
I want to show you all the things I can do. There's nothing to be afraid of...

CHARLIE
Get away from me. Oh God... No.

TIM has hold of CHARLIE and is trying to pull him out of the bed.

TIM
Soon you'll be like me, Charlie. And I know you'll love it. I can see behind me, I can fly. We're going to be like our Dad...

CHARLIE screams.
RONNIE wakes. She leaps out of bed and runs into CHARLIE'S bedroom space. We are in close. TIM has climbed right on top of his brother and is trying to lift him out of bed. CHARLIE continues to shout.

RONNIE
Tim, leave him!

As TIM turns, CHARLIE scrambles away. Now TIM begins to advance on his mother. Fearfully, she backs away.

RONNIE
Tim, you know who I am...

TIM
Yes, you're the one who killed my father...

RONNIE
It wasn't like that. He was in terrible pain, he was dying.

TIM stretches out a suckered hand towards his mother. Fluid from his jaws oozes to the floor and sizzles on the bare wood. It looks like he could do RONNIE real harm.

TIM
I'm not going to let you destroy me or Charlie.

The sucker attaches itself to RONNIE'S cheek and TIM holds her there.

CHARLIE
Don't hurt her! Get away from her!

TIM
We have to be what we really are now...
Don't try to stop us.

Her terror affects the remaining human part of him. He relents. He lets her go. She drops to the floor, clutching at her face. GUNTHER appears in the door. They watch in silence as TIM scales the wall and retreats into the rafters.

Ian McEwan's latest novel, *Saturday*, will be filmed with a screenplay by Patrick Marber.

Frederic Raphael

In Earlier Episodes

When recruited as a mercenary, Guy Fielden does not *wish* to be captured, tortured, executed, but he entertains a constant fantasy that he will be. Fear does not inhibit appetite; it is part of it. At school, two decades earlier, he watched, and winced as the headmonitor laid into a bent boy. Fielden now feels complicity with Major Farrer, the leader of the mercenaries to which he has been recruited 'for good money'. He is amused to call Farrer 'Kurtz' to those who do not take the reference.

Farrer assumes unforgivable qualities. He makes no apology; he lives his choices. Fielden envies the Major's lack of conscience. Infatuated with what he cannot be, he smiles, somewhat, at the Major's question after burning and shooting: 'Now who's for dinner?'

Once a choirboy, Fielden's *imitatio* is not of Christ Himself, but of the robbers crucified with Him: he dreams of being the other felon (paired with Farrer) in the crucifixion. His schoolboy Christianity craved 'purity', the symptom of corruption.

Nathan Bailey is a solicitor specialising in tax affairs. Nathan honours Sartre in 'assuming' his Jewishness: he agrees to be what he cannot escape being, by choosing to inhabit an identity wished on him by others. One can decide to be only what one is not. Such an existential decision implies a vestigial, colourless self which chooses the role to enact.

Nathan (let others spot the Lessing allusion) enjoys a life of earned propriety. He assists others to avoid tax, but only by breaching the spirit of the law while remaining within the letter. He himself honours the spirit as well. A cook who never swallows his best recipes, he shuns his own schemes.

Nathan has written standard works on Tax Law. He contributes irregularly on legal/ethical issues to *The Statesman*. He takes part in lucrative seminars and also in *pro bono* 'surgeries'. At his offices in Lordship Lane, he counsels working-class tenants threatened with eviction by landlords who can make more money cramming blacks into the same premises.

Nathan's blameless addiction is duplicate bridge. His regular partner, Roy Carn, is a man whose private life (wife, mistresses, and hints of orgies) amuses him, though such a diet is not for him. His and Carn's tournament successes have earned them hopes of selection for the England team. Their system is Baronised Acol; oh, and ace from ace-king.

Nathan is asked by HMG to go to Southern Rhodesia to intercede for three Africans condemned to death by the Smith regime. He has already appeared for them in front of the judicial commitee of the Privy Council. It ordained the men's reprieve; an empty grace, since all knew that the Salisbury regime would never honour it. Congratulated in the street (quietly) by junior minister in the Foreign Office, Nathan said, 'Now you can look forward to the executions, is that it?'

The man said, 'You're a cynic, Mr Bailey.'

Nathan said, 'Ask not for whom the ball rolls.'

'Do I follow?'

'Do you not?'

'Is something vexing you?'

'Should it not?'

'We won, Mr Bailey. Thanks to you. The appeal.'

'Your neck is safe, you mean?'

'Look on the bright side: and your OBE, I shouldn't wonder, Mr Bailey.'

When the execution date is confirmed, HMG asks him, as a favour he need not of course grant, to go to Salisbury and 'see what can be done'. He told Roy Carn (because the date of an imminent Gold Cup match would have to be changed), 'I'm HMG's new-style gun-boat: no gun.'

He and Roy stand to be picked for England as replacements for a pair recently accused of cheating, at the European Championships, by using pre-arranged finger signals to indicate length in spades. If Hatton and Matheson are adjudged guilty at the coming inquiry, Nathan and Roy are the obvious choice.

Nathan is then asked by the English Bridge Union to represent the accused couple before the tribunal. If he succeeds on their behalf, the 'suspended' pair will be re-instated. The gap in the England ranks will be closed to Nathan and Carn. That, more than any belief in their innocence, makes Nathan fervent in his defence of the accused.

When they met again, years after being at school together, Fielden congratulated Nathan on being unmarked by the painful weeks he endured. As a senior fellow-scholar, Fielden observed 'hooky' Nathan's petty calvary, without either participating or doing anything to arrest it. He did leave a book in Nathan's cubicle: Auden's *The Age of Anxiety*. 'Would you believe that I envied you?'

One of the accused players, Harold Hatton, is renowned for tall acidity. 'No one likes H H...' The other accused, Ira Sherman, is said, by one of the 'reluctant' accusers, to have confessed: 'It was all that man H H's idea. I was fool enough to go along with it.'

Ira swears to Nathan that he never said any such thing, and then that he certainly never meant it 'as a confession'.

'Then what?'

'I added something they omitted. Deliberately.'

'You added it deliberately; or they omitted it deliberately?'

'You're enjoying this. They omitted that I said, "That's what you want me to say, isn't it?" Because that was what they said they would "accept". Bloody Beamish hates H H even more than they hate me. Happy now?'

'Happy...'

'I know: you think I'm a shit. I fuck people's wives. Doesn't Roy Carn?'

'Is this bus going anywhere relevant?'

'I know your game, Nathan. The straight man never wins.'

'Some things are more important than winning.'

'Get out of my team.'

How does Ira not having an accent come to be an accent?

'I want to ask you why H H didn't seem in the least ... indignant when you were accused. "Unsurprised" is how Master Beamish describes him in his affidavit.'

'Not that you could see,' Sherman said. 'What's indignation to you? Yelling and blustering and blubbing? Me too, old cock. But H H expected this to happen one day. He probably even wanted it. Bloody virgin.'

'H H? I thought he was married.'

'It amuses him: to take the unexpected as if he expected it. Bastard. It doesn't me. H H never blinks when a suit breaks badly. They discuss hands is all they do, in bed. He and cunty.'

'I'm on your side, Ira.'

'If we'd cheated, we'd've won by a street. No one could've touched us. We didn't, and we didn't. End of case.'

'If you don't wreck it yourself. I don't know why people are so willing to come and testify on your behalf, but they are.'

'Blow-flies,' Ira said. 'You can hear the buzz.'

'Jean-Marc admits he doesn't like you, either of you. For some reason...'

'I fucked his wife. Everyone knows that.'

'Good news. He's still prepared to say, after analysing the hands, that you didn't cheat. He insists it would've been bound to show up in the results of the boards in question and it doesn't. You did untypically badly on several of them.'

'I played like a cunt,' Ira said. 'You're not a bad chap, Nathan.'

'I can't help that.'

'Poor man! If only we were guilty, there'd be some satisfaction for you in getting us off.'

Thanks mainly to Jean-Marc Grolegeac's hand-by-hand analysis, the accused pair were adjudged not guilty. The panel did not, however, indicate that they found the charges unthinkable. Nathan's advocacy had, it seemed, succeeded in disqualifying himself and Roy Carn for the England team.

Nathan is married to a lapsed Catholic. Mary is shackled to the shade of a faith in which she no longer has belief, somewhat as Nathan is to Judaism. One of their sons, Christopher, was born with spina bifida. The other now runs a fish restaurant in San Diego where no reservations are taken. His line is always busy.

Nathan does *pro bono* work at the request of the government, more readily when he thinks little of the party in power. He also acts occasionally for Christian Aid and Oxfam. Mary read French and Spanish at Somerville. She knew Guy Fielden there. He introduced her to Nathan.

Before he met Mary, Nathan had a long affair with a woman who, as a child, had been in a concentration camp. Marta asked specific things of him which loving her inhibited him from doing. She provoked his jealousy as an incitement to punish her. When he refused, she detailed what a less squeamish man had been happy to do, and showed him the marks. She smiled (but never laughed) at his rage, and then at his tears. Nathan has never quarrelled with Mary, nor wept over her.

On the eve of the executions, Nathan was asked by the Secretary of State to fly to Salisbury to plead in person for mercy. On arrival, he told the local press that he was confident that the illegal government, which paraded itself as truer to British traditions than modern Britain herself, would not ignore a judicial decision taken in London. Privately, he recognised that he had been sent to Salisbury to prove that London had done everything possible to save men whose execution would warrant the British government's isolation of the Smith regime rather better than their reprieve.

His plea for mercy is heard with the parodic courtesy to be expected from judges already determined to reject it. A break-down in the air conditioning shortens everybody's breath. The chief justice apologises, Mr Bailey, for the discomfort, especially for someone so unfamiliar with African conditions.

From his hotel room, Nathan telephoned his wife to make sure that she was all right. Knowing that the call was being monitored, he spoke French to her. It lent his voice a particular warmth.

He then found, in the Salisbury directory, the number of a couple, Gerry and Sybil Pye, whom he had met some years before on a bridge cruise. They had invited him to come and 'visit us in paradise'.

'Gerry Pye?'

'Who is this?' Gerry says.

'Nathan. Bailey. How are you? How's Sybil?'

'I heard you were here, you kaffir-loving Jew bastard. I'm very sorry you called. Don't ever do it again.'

Nathan hangs up, happy. To be a pariah is rejuvenating.

Unable to sleep, he left the hotel and walked the streets. Was he being followed? Did he see himself being beaten up by 'unknown' assaailants?

On Independence Avenue, he is solicited by a black whore. She has pink heels.

In her sour room, he asks if she ever whipped people. 'You like me to do that to you, boss? I will.' He agrees to pay her more.

He has her do it in the same posture he was forced to take at school. The whipping does not excite him; it hurts. After she has hit him a few times, he asks her to stop. Would she object to 'something else'? It would have to be extra. 'Of course'. He has blackmailed himself.

He then asks her to bend over the chair as he had. The present is his past. He contemplates the black rump, the liverish slit below it. He remains clammy with impotence. She looks back at him. He shakes his head and lies on the bed. He cannot please even himself.

'Don't blame Sophie, boss, will you?'

'No, no.' He escapes the room as if a cell. 'Thank you, Sophie.'

He walks back to the Royal Salisbury Palace hotel, shuddering in the night heat. Is he followed? He throws himself on the bed without undoing his shoes: black on white. He wakes, awake at seven. The three men are to be hanged at eight. He tells himself to leave the room and go down to breakfast. He has given himself a present to be ashamed of: Sophie.

He lay on the rumpled bed and, as the fatal hour grew closer, comforted himself. Marta, Marta. He came at the same time as the black men at the end of their ropes.

Nathan's government-sponsored trip to Rhodesia pre-dates, by several years, his private mission to save Guy Fielden from the regime of Winston Churchill ('That is what I choose to be called'). Winston Churchill was at Sandhurst; he wears a British-style uniform, Sam Browne, droop of tasselled lanyards, red tabs.

The People's Democratic Republic has the power (and unquestionable evidence) to condemn Farrer, Fielden and the other mercenaries. This time, no Privy Council has gone through the antics of reprieve. Nathan goes to Fielden's aid without the diplomatic sanction which, ten years before, protected and stigmatised him. HMG cannot be seen to connive with mercenaries.

This time, Nathan's only sponsor in London is the long-fingered Piet (Peeety) Petersen ('my e is short, unlike my temper') who sponsored the Major's 'botched, but we mustn't say so' expedition. Nathan has had previous tangential contact with Petersen, who has 'rented' one of his 'kosher, they tell me' tax shelters. Petersen has complicated origins. 'I have several fathers, Mr Bailey, isn't it? That's how I learnt to diversify. And to take the long view along with the short e.'

Nathan's father's name was not Bailey. He agrees to be charmed by Petersen, one of whose fathers left Holland for Argentina in 1945.

'Major Farrer is by way of being my man,' Petersen says. 'Save his bacon and I'll take exceptionally good care of you.'

'I'm not doing it for...that kind of reason.'

'No? Disinterested nobility may be wasted on friend Farrer.'

'I was at school with one of his men. Guy Fielden.'

'Close friend?'

'Close enemy.'

'Love and hate, old chums!'

Nathan wonders why Petersen and his associates contacted him. While having a 'strictly private word', board member Lord Bromwich assures him that he recommended Nathan to 'Peety P' as the one man who, on form, can help Fielden (and the Major). 'I remember you going to Salisbury years ago.'

'They hanged the three men I was representing.'

'Thing being, Bailey, the Group has important interests adjacent to friend Winston's little playground. We don't want him unduly provoked.'

'I doubt if I have the resources to provoke anyone, duly or unduly.'

'Good man. Massage massah is more the line. Grovel even, if you can bring yourself, for the good of the company.'

'I was given to believe I'm strictly on a mercy mission.'

'It's a tricky one, but the hand can be played. Allow me to suggest finesse rather than squeeze.'

'You're a bridge player!' Nathan said.

'No, you are. My game is being well-informed.'

Bromwich opened a door and startled a slim woman in a black linen suit (keenly creased trousers) leaning over a map. Adjacent to her, a man on a black leather swivel chair, with pale freckles and improbable red hair, was bracing his neck against folded hands.

'Oh sorry,' Bromwich said, and closed the door. 'Bloody doors all look the same. Today's architecture. I rather think we wanted this one.'

Winston Churchill's province was once a British colony. Lawyers continue to wear wigs as they plead in its rigged trials. Winston finds it prudent to go through the motions of British judicial nicety, so long as they turn no wheels.

Nathan is given more respect in Uhuru City than he was in Salisbury: everyone shakes hands and smiles. He suspects, but must not acknowledge, that other plans are in train. The woman in the black linen suit and the man with improbable hair are at the breakfast buffet when he comes down one morning.

'What the hell are you doing here?'

'What are you, Guy?'

'Seeking salvation, aren't I?'

'In curious company.'

'Only place to find it. Sorry about this dump. Don't be surprised if you see a rat.'

'I want to get you out of here.'

'Why?'

'Oh for God's sake.'

'*Lawless Roads*,' Guy Fielden says. 'Read it at the wrong age. And here I am. And here you are, wasting your time. They'll almost certainly shoot me whatever you do.'

'Let's cling to the "almost" aspect.'

Fielden grinned, as if at the past. He was Hamlet to Nathan's Polonius in a school play. 'How about if I came here knowing we'd be caught?'

'Is that why you're so...calm?'

'Try"amused".'

'You should wake up, Guy, and realise this isn't... a play.'

'Isn't it? Of course it is. Pack of cards. Did you ever read Nabokov's *Invitation to a Beheading*?'

'I don't have anything in common with you, Guy. I realise that now. Nothing.'

'That's why we love each other the way we do. Or do we?'

'Not a love I recognise.'

'Those are the ones, Nathan, those are the ones! How fat a fee did they pay you to come and prostrate yourself before big Winnie the definitive pooh? You can tell an old friend.'

'When I have one, I will. What persuaded you to be a mercenary? You wouldn't even join the bloody Corps!'

'Same difference, as the oiks say. You want to lord it over me as I once did over you, don't you? Save me as I never did you. Only I have to be in a state of terror for that to work, hence your disappointment that I'm not. Fury. Hidden, but fury.'

'They're going to stage a public execution.'

'Howls of execration? Camus's *L'Etranger*. One of my favourites.'

'I'm not an examiner, Guy, and this isn't bloody Oxford. Stop showing knowledge. I propose to tell them Farrer misled you. And that you'll give evidence against him. Why shake your head?'

'Because I won't. And it wouldn't work if I did. The Major is far more Winston's kind of a chap than I am.'

'Let me tell them you might. He's the villain, and they must know it.'

'They do. That's how they know he's the goods.'

'And he'll save his own skin if he can, and to hell with Guy Fielden.'

'Good for him. Always was my destination. Why are you standing up?'

'I may as well go home.'

'Oh stay and see me shot, do. I shall only be offended.'

'Fuck you, Guy, honestly.'

'You didn't think Mary was a virgin, did you, when you married her?'

'Perhaps I bloody well will stay.'

Nathan lies on his bed in the low hotel. The fan stirs the fat air like tepid soup. Black bugs crawl on the sheet. Damn Guy Fielden to hell. Or somewhere.

Winston Churchill sends an adjutant with word that he is prepared to meet Nathan. He will send his official Mercedes.

'You will call him "Highest Excellency",' the adjutant tells Nathan as he is shown into the gilded room in what was once Government House. There is a bellied refrigerator in the corner, with a downward handle.

'You are a Jew, Mr Bailey?'

'Rather, Most Excellency.'

'Highest, Mr Bailey, Highest Highest.'

'I beg your pardon, sir.'

'You are here why?'

'Because, Highest Excellency...'

'Top man.'

'...Guy Fielden, one of Major Farrer's minor players...'

'Minor players, good!'

'...is an old friend of mine. I am here to beg for him to be shown mercy, Highest Excellency.'

'A Christian Jew! The Israelis are my best friends, you know.

Wonderful machine-guns. No questions asked. I also know Peety P, in Geneva. A real man.'

'I assure you...'

'Good. Very good indeed. You came off your own bat. Most excellent! And Peety lent you his pads! You want to take Mr Fielding home with you?'

'I'd like to do that very much.'

'Big game! Sling him across your bumpers, white hunter. White hunter is you. So do it. Tell them you argued me, you begged me and Mr Churchill showed that he is a gracious man. Goodness gracious. I watch TV, you know. Old films. Everything.'

'Would you...Highest Excellency...'

'Of course, of course.'

'Write me a line authorising me to...?'

'I will shoot you a line. Your friend is a free man. And you didn't give me a penny, did you? I want your Queen, our Queen, to come and pay me a visit.'

'I don't think I can promise that, Highest Excellency.'

'But it will happen.'

Winston Churchill takes a gold pen, thick as a carrot, and signs a piece of paper on his desk. He passes it to Nathan. It is an order to the prison governor to release Guy Fielden to Nathan Bailey's personal custody.

'Sorry if I've spoiled your plans.'

'What makes you think you have?'

'You're not going to be shot, are you?'

'Perhaps that was never the plan.' Guy's grin is an unwanted gift.

'Whose plan?'

'There's the rub. You've heard of Hamlet presumably?'

'Did you know all along that it was never going to happen? I thought you were...oh all right...Meursault if you want. And you were... something else, weren't you? What?'

Guy Fielden clapped Nathan on the shoulder, as if claiming him. '*Ca, c'est mon petit bagage, mon vieux.*'

Back in London, Petersen and Lord Bromwich propose to give Nathan a large sum of money, in Geneva if he wants.

'I don't want a thing. I'm only sorry about the Major.'

'Oh don't be. Don't be.'

A week later, he sees on the television that Winston Churchill has found no evidence that Major Farrer was in his country for any malign purpose whatsoever. His arrest was, Winston Churchill tells CNN, 'purely precautionary. I am now completely satisfied.' The Major has been appointed Winston Churchill's chief of security. A groundbreaking (as Piet Petersen calls it at the same press conference) agreement has been brokered for International Resources Group to be an equal partner with the Democratic People's Republic in exploring potentially rich new mines on the border of the neighouring state. 'We mean it to be a model for the new Africa.'

When Nathan tells Roy Carn the story, Carn reminds him of Jean-Marc's dictum: the cheat is revealed only by results which defy the odds to be expected in straight dealing.

Nathan calls Marta.

Copyright Volatic Ltd 2006

Frederic Raphael's latest book is *Some Talk of Alexander: A Journey Through Space and Time in the Greek World*, published by Thames and Hudson.

Peter Sansom

The Wife of Bath's Tale
as retold by Gladys Ruth Sansom (86) of Sutton-in-Ashfield, Notts.

Never had much time for Charlie, but he's all reight to talk to. Day he come, fost thing he said was he wor fair clammed. Mrs, he said, me stomach thinks me throat's cut. I said well it's bread and drippin, else you'll have to do like they do in Sheffield. He said what's that (never been to Sheffield, only to visit). I said, Do wi'ert. He laughed and said bread and drippin it is then.

    Bread and drippin! As if folks'd give royalty bread and drippin! Our Joss'd oppened a tin of ham. It wor all done ready in kitchen under a teatowel. He worn't on his own, the Prince, nayther. We had a houseload, and it's not a big flat, them as look after him and such, and them for the telly, and they all wanted snap and a cup of tea.

    After he'd had a bite, he said, Well Mrs, you know why we're here. I said Aye I do an'all, but it's not me as you want, you want Clara Do-Rose. He looked at me gone-out, But you're a widder three times ovver, and my man here said that you know. I said that's as may be, but it's Clara Do Rose as you want. She knows. She can give you your answer. Well, Clara knows what women want, and no bogger'd argue with Clara. Mind, I've not seen her since the war. There was that yank, Doodle Bug we christened him on account of his tash, but she stuck by her Malcolm, with his foot blown off, even though he was neither use nor ornament, never wanted no bogger looking at his foot, even Clara, even in the dark. Well it don't figure for me, me duck, she told him, but it were no good, might as well tek a dolly to bed. Even then give her her due, she never let Doodle Bug do as he liked more than twice else three times, and she were drunk as a lord one of them as I know to, because I were wi' her in a car one of them old uns like you don't see now. It worn't his, we just saw it parked up, and it were bitter cold and they didn't lock up in them days so he said, let's gerrin here for a warm. I were in front with, now who wor I wi'? Clara and Doodle Bug wor in back, hardly got started when door oppens and it's this Captain whose car it wor.

Anyroad. Next item on the agenda it's Clara hersen, he must have had her sent for. Never thought to see her in my house. She'd changed. I said, I'd not know you Clara. And I wouldn't, not with that hair, she had lovely hair. Grow it another couple of inch, you could sit on your hair, that's what her Malcolm said. What would I want to sit on me hair for, she said, me arse'll do me for sitting on. If there's anything wants growing by two inch, Malcolm Dodd, you know where it's billeted. Grow that and I'll sit on it for you. He went bright red, it was in the tap room of the Traveller's, and we were all theer. She didn't care, Clara. I wonder Malcolm didn't land her one, and I think she'd warrant it some nights specially when we'd been out on the qv, but he didn't have the means. Aye, you *do* me lad, you so much as offer, she said, and I'll box your bleedin blindin ears. She had a mouth on her, did Clara, but she had a right hook too. I don't hold with language, not for women anyroad, but she didn't have no choice, he was always so boggering sorry for his-sen, Malcolm.

Anyroad up, the Prince says he'll have another if there's one in the pot and now Clara's here we can get started. Nice manners, but you expect that of royalty. You don't notice his ears so much to his face. But it worn't Clara Do-Rose, not with that hair and her bent double like a safety pin. That worn't the Clara I knew, any bogger could see it worn't her, but I thought if it meks him happy good luck to him, and it did because she says 'Yes,' she says, 'I can tell you, and I'm the only one as can'.

The prince said, 'You can?' Room went quiet: well, it matters, this, to him. Because his mam's had this message from God in the middle of doing a jigsaw of their house, about handing on the reins or throwing the towel in for good. She said God had said, Let Charles tek ovver now lass, only you've got to set him a test fost. She says

What's that then God? He says, There's more women in your country than men, and it's not reight as things stand, women should have more say. So for a start your lad Charles has to tell you what it is that women want. And this answer, what women want, it's got to be an answer that not one woman in the country'd disagree wi'. Either he tells you that or he don't get the kingdom, no bogger does, because it's going to be one of them like France or America where they don't have no royalty. Tell him he's got a year and a day, God says. Then he thinks again and says, Nay, with all this helicopters and satellites and such tell him he's got a week.

So Charles, he goes rushin round like a blue-arsed fly. Asking everybogger. Archbishop of Canterbury, Chief of Police, Lionel Blair. Then he has a brainwave and asks his dad, what he thinks it is his mum wants. Apparently Philip says, I don't know as she wants owt, lad, she's not short of a bob or two. But he's been tipped the wink that Charles has to ask a widder three times ovver living round our way. In a council flat. Course that's me, and here we are. But it worn't me.

And Clara Do-Rose, or her as says she's Clara Do-Rose, says again, 'Yes, and I'm the only bogger on God's earth as *can* tell you.' And it wor reight quiet, as I say, apart from the chuntering of them cameras. Then she says, 'I'll tell you summat for nowt, though, that sort of information don't come cheap.' Now Clara's Malcolm wor like that, so mean he wouldn't let you light a candle off his lamp; but not Clara. She were always oppenhanded. We'd say, Clara you'll never have no money so long as you've a hole in your arse. And bonny, she wor proper bonny, and now I think on she wor a lot like that wife of his what killed hersen or ran off with a foreigner, I know it wor summat o' sort. Car crash that wor it, I think. I do know they took snooker off. Nowt on telly, Joss said, that Princess Dinah's died. Aye, it wor a long day that one.

But this Clara Do-Rose, when she said that about it not coming cheap, well she looked just like one of them what-do-you-call-its. I'm not joking. Manny and mardarse at same time. Charlie says: Mrs, you can name your price.

Door went just then. It wor our Joss, he'd been out for more milk. They'd only got sterra, he says, and, By, it's a top coat warmer out theer. And he stops, cos cameras's going. But this is what they want, the news men. Cameras going and it's all lit up for the telly. I'll mash some tea, he says, and he goes.

She says I don't want no money. There's this pause. And she says, 'I want him'. And she points at this young feller as is with the prince. Not long out of school, by the looks on it. 'Not married, are you me duck?' she says and he laughs but she's not laughing.

Sorry Mrs, the prince says, Sir Dooins is not for sale, ask for anything, what do you want: wealth, jewellery, a palace ...

She says, I've always fancied owning a race horse. And Charlie's face lights up. But no, she says, only Sir Dooins here will do, his hand in marriage. She grins her one-tooth at him, and gives him this wink. Charlie tells the telly men to turn their tackle off and bogger off out onto the landing.

When they've gone, Sir Dooins says Mrs, I will marry you whenever you wish.

Charlie says you'll do no such thing Gerald or Jason or whatever his name is. And this lad says But Your Highness, it's not for my country, I'm doing it for you. I thought he wor going to cry, the prince, he wor that moved. You can hear the clock going now, too big for the room. Charlie sits reight still for a bit like he's thinking reight hard, says summat quiet to the lad, who nods, and then says summat else quiet to the man with the briefcase, and this man says, We'll have one of them contracts drawn up.

Nay, says Clara, we don't need no contracts. If you agree here and now to wed me, no lawyer'll wangle you out on it, not in this world. What do you say? And the lad, this Sir Dooins, says alright and they shake hands, 'I do this for the Prince'. Clara says (and you've got to remember she's 70, nay she'll be 80-odd) she says, Give ovver, it's nowt to do with him, you can't help yoursen can you? Men, you're all the same, led ovver the fields by your willy-nilly.

Not fields though, now, it's all built up round that way. Tek the precinct. I remember when it was Idlewells, though I lived out at Bleak Hall in them days, Tod's Row it wor called then. Oh yes, tell you who I went to school wi' as you'll know: Harold Larwood. Pub named for him now up Annesley. It'd surprise if me dad isn't in there this minute, though I can't tell you the last time he called round here. It's a few years. A good few years since I've seen me dad. I don't know where he is these days tell the truth. He said, don't you worry, you can take your hat off, Fanny Ann, I can see you've had your hair cut. He never wanted me to have me hair cut, didn't me dad. Finest fast bowler England ever had and he might just as well have not bothered if you ask anybogger. Harold Larwood. Harold Larwood, George Formby, you don't hear nowt on them nowadays, Dr Steiney, you never see him nayther. Nor our Tony.

So they call back the telly men and set the cameras going for what all women want. Even with all that you can still hear the clock ticking and everybogger holding their breath. Well? the prince says. Hold your hosses, Clara says, you've got to stand up and ask me reight. So the Prince of Wales stands up in my living room and says, Mrs Do-Rose, Tell us now what it is that all women want. And she smiles. You'll notice my fiance there, he's got lovely big hands, she says, and it's true what they say I can tell you, she says, and that's one of the reasons I decided he wor for me. Women don't want a man for decoration.

But nay, I'm only teasing, that's not it, or not all there is to it, not by a long chalk. Anyroad she says, What women want, it's what you'd expect. And she pauses like. Then: women want to be in charge of their-sens. After a moment Charlie nods, Ay, he says, to be their own boss, like, happen you're right. Me mam'll agree with that I should think. And well, as you know, she does agree an all, and we're into all this parliament rigmarole.

But then it's not a week later, and it's the wedding isn't it in London. I don't go, not with this leg, but I see it on telly like everybogger else. Well Clara's a sight. Old enough to be his grandma and falling down drunk even at the altar, and when it comes to her vows she says I f-in well do and laughs so you can see she's not reight in head.

All ovver bar the shoutin, I think, when who should come round next day but Charles again, and on his own an all.

Well, we've got nowt in house and it's days since Joss went round with the ewbank, but he says he's not stoppin. So Joss mashes a pot of tea and finds out a packet of fig biscuits and half a layer of teatime assorted. The prince has brought some photos of the happy couple (that's what he called them). Seems as Clara made him bring them for old time's sake. And in the photos it really is Clara Do-Rose. I mean the Clara as was. Beautiful. I couldn't believe it. Charlie pours another cup and tells me how it's come about, which is this: After the wedding, they went somewhere posh for the reception, and after somewhere grand for the wedding night. Well this Sir Dooins, he's a perfect gentleman and even though she's nasty, I mean not just to look at, I mean nasty in hersen, mardy and allus on, like one of them little dogs that pees up your sofa because it can't sink its teeth in your leg. Nevermind that, he's lovely with her all the same. But that's him, Charles says, that's him, generous in his heart, like one of the old-fashioned knights, the knights of the round table, I forget which one he said. It worn't Albert I do know.

And on his wedding night, just as it's dropping dark, he's looking out across at the gardens to the river reight far off, just stood theer, Sir Dooins, at his winder, a bit worried obviously. In comes his bride. He hears but don't turn round at fost. But it's Clara like in the photo, the beautiful Clara Do-Rose, nineteen else twenty. Clara Do-Rose at nineteen. She could pass for nineteen till she wor 30, as a matter of fact, them nights we went singing down the Market Tavern and the Soldiers and Sailors, the Traveller's Rest, the Dog and Duck, the Staff of Life, touring round. When a song come on the wireless we liked we'd write it down on a sugar bag and practice in front room and go out of a night and sing for us larrup till chucking-out time, pissed up, Malcolm never objected nor mine. So this is Clara as she wor when I knew her. When he turns to her, Sir Dooins can't believe his eyes. This isn't the woman he wed. Ah but it is, she says, I'm Clara Do-Rose reight enough.

And this is it: because you loved me, because you saw into who I wor, this is who I am tonight on our wedding night. Well they hug each other, like they would. Then she steps back. But, she says, you've got to choose. I can be like this, and young as I am now, for only half the time. At night or else in the day. Before or after sunset I have to be the old Clara Do Rose again. Which is it to be, my husband, she says, old by day or in your bed?

(Joss worn't taking it in at all; he said, They're closing that Kwiksave. Are they really, his Highness says. He's alright, he'll just go down the precinct like he used to. They've finished the precinct, done it up, put a roof on it, made a nice job on it an all.)

Anyroad where wor I? Yes. So Sir Dooins has to choose, day or night. She says, Clara does, 'You've got till tomorrer to mek your mind up.' Quick as a flash he says I don't need till tomorrer me duck. I know what my answer is. Clara interrupts, Ayup lad be careful now, I know you men, thrice nightly fost week and it's off down the allotment theerafter – don't you be hasty. Sir Dooins raises his hand. Nay, Mrs, he says, I said I know what my answer is and I'm sticking to it: young by day or young by night, that's for *you* to decide.

Now the prince gets excited telling this and the bottom half of his bourbon's come away in his tea. This is the best part he says, it's like a fairy story, he says because Clara Do-Rose when she hears him say that she's reight glad because now she can be young all the time, and she is. You see, it's like brokken a spell, him saying as it's up to her, seeing as she's her own boss.

I say, So they live happily ever after then do they? Looks like it, he says. And what about you, your highness, I say, you get to be king now do you? He sets off on it but I stop him, I don't need to know all the ins and outs o' Meg's arse. There's the door and it'll be our Maureen and Diane or our Maureen and Mick. But it's me dad. Oh dad, I've fair missed you, I say, I can't think of owt else. And he sits there, large as life, still wi' his boots on. You'll never guess, he says, who I've just been talking wi'. But I know, I don't know how: Harold Larwood, I say, and it wor an all, took the wind out on his sails. But ayup father, can you see we've got company? Dad, this is the Prince of Wales. Your Highness, this is me dad. And I didn't know where to put mesen because me dad just said, I can see that, and what's it to me: I only died for such as him. And happen he did because the prince said, Mester, I know as you did, I do know that very well. And they shake hands. By it wor a sight, as if they wor the same man underneath. Well they wor, and that's a thought, your dad and your king as will be, your dad and your king the same man, it struck me all of a sudden. And both on 'em beholden, beholden to me or my kind, and me and my kind beholden to them an all, or to him and his kind, if you follow me, that's how it is. Living or dead, woman or man, then or nar.

Peter Sansom is Director of the Poetry Business and editor of The North and Smith/Doorstop Books. His own publications include *Writing Poems* (Bloodaxe), *January* and *Point of Sale* (both from Carcanet).

Veronica Horwell

In Guatemala

In the autumn and winter of 1989, I served an apprenticeship in making journeys. I followed the Santa Fe trail from Independence, Missouri, through to New Mexico, turning South along the Chihuahua trail, and then took the old Camino Real route across Central America. For many years I looked longingly in books at the traditional textiles of places along the route, inspired assertions of indigenous identities – at Navajo rugs, Saltillo serapes, Tehuantepec embroideries, and most of all at the Mayan clothes of the highlands of Guatemala.

Guatemala was logged as having the world's worst human rights record for the year 1989.

Zunil, Guatemala. Bus drivers had touted for passengers like fairground barkers in the depot in Quetzaltenango, Xela City. I meant to catch a fresh transport to the market in blankets at Momostenango but instead boarded at random the usual ex-US-school-bus. The driver's seat was velvet-draped in hearse mode. He had shouted that his destination was Zunil, Zunil.

On the way there his bus grudged and edged past a village where treadle loom workshops produced some of the world's wittiest textiles, stripes and checkers marbled with ikat, worn by the entire length as skirts and aprons: pleated, gathered, frilled, as much yardage as could be afforded. Massive stemmed arum lilies jammed every ditch. We turned – a triple oblique zigzag – down to Zunil, making an extra zag to avoid conquistadores in carved masks, prancing to drum and pipe, in the plaza before the church.

Down below, the river Samala sped, swollen and swept along by rainwater from the hills. Far up, between the green and each mountain cone's personal cloud, women were descending the paths. Their feet slapped. From the side of roads through the highlands I had watched how every straw and thread root was picked and swept from the tiny milpa fields after a crop. The soil, soft as house dust, was near sieved clean, then mounded by hoes for the next planting. Paths were a bare foot wide, not to waste good growing ground. They had never conceded to the wheel. People trod lightly on them. The earth supported vegetables: in Zunil, cabbages, potatoes, avocadoes, all handled courteously.

Fruit was treated even more respectfully than the vegetables. In the plaza, a woman bought one holiday orange for several children. The stall-holder inserted it in a old metal contraption that spiralled off the rind. He halved it and knifed on salt and chilli. Each child got a couple of sucks and a bite, watching the dancers.

Festive ropes were tied to the bell-towers of the whitewashed church, and secured to a post in the plaza. It might have been a liner, hawsered, the holy statues in their niches waving bon voyage. The church door was shut. A firework boomed. It opened. Men on one side, women the other, the congregation stood on the steps. The door was secured again quickly, shutting in paper banners to our patroness St Catherine. Her altar was silver, solid, Spanish.

Eating tables were set up inside a rough tent comida. A fat woman who ran it tended half a dozen elemental stoves of logs, barely red for a slow braise.

What's in the pot?

Flesh.

What flesh?

Chicken. Turkey.

Ma'am Jefe [the boss], was served by two small handmaidens in flounces. They had filled an oil drum with water by walking to the fountain half a mile away with plastic amphorae on their heads, a few pints per trip. Zunil had had drinkable water, at last, in 1984, thanks to benefactors listed on a plaque on the fountain. Its secondary function was to act as a grandstand. I was taller than the crowd and did not need its lift to see the Mayan hero, Tecan Uman – feather-crowned, carrying bow and arrows – dancing in token resistance against masked Spaniards, the Alvarado crew. Their cloaks flashed with tin and mirrors. Their wooden faces exaggerated European features into surreality – eyebrows a spread eagle or confronted hawks. A second team of dancers – red-coated soldiers with vestigial dispatch pouches – went on to the playing area. They did not always jig, but sometimes sat on chairs in the square, mimed smoking and drinking, wagging their fingers in no local gesture. Plumed princesses watched as a third file, blonde-bearded, clashed swords with the Spanish. They had bicorne hats athwart Admiral's rigs and were pirates – or the British navy, remembered as the same thing.

Dance of pirates with muskets.

The conquistadores re-entered.

So it went on. At the end of the morning, a rival team started up a clarinet for a Mexican dance. The charro costume was wickedly pastiched: for hours through the afternoon, as thunder sounded from the peaks, a few phrases were repeatedly struck on the marimba. The 'maiden's' brown, dry, male wrists never stopped lifting 'her' skirt. By three we were due for a downpour and enough liquor had been drunk for dancers to stagger. Two bussed-in rival sound systems crackled at each other. One sound system was for salsa (such amplification was appreciated). Flocks of girls, a few albinos with white eyelashes, perched on the church steps and watched El Grupo Salsa with a sha-nah-nah trio backing. But a bigger audience got up for the brass band, which would try anything and did fine with Glenn Miller.

Yet another group of maskers came circling. Two dogs. A pair of cowboys. One and a half Chinamen, early Aladdin panto pattern. Grey masks of Europeans. An unmatched set of spacemen, one with a motorbike helmet and a vampire mask, the other in a knight's visor.

Any faces but their own.

'In The Mood' and 'Chattanooga Choo-Choo' got louder and louder, until the other groups in the plaza had to perform without being able to hear their instruments.

A hailstorm. Then fireworks like a hailstorm.

The amps shorted and were restored.

One dancer at a time retired for a shot of booze or to adjust ecru tights simulating the un-naturalness of Spanish hose.

It was more than the effortful happiness of holiday. Those circles, round and round, rewound time, tensed its spring. Without this output of energy, some year the cycles might not restart.

The plaza steps were saturated in purple and red as the women sat in threes and fives, arms around each other. Beautiful crowds with filthy feet. At first in Mayan territory I had only been able to identify the clothes, *traje*, of the marcador towns – San Antonio Aguas Calientes, Comalapa, Chichicastenengo. The brocade weavers there followed coloured, squared-up charts – originally designed for cross-stitching roses, bluebirds, pansies – to create their upper garments, *huipiles*. The machine-embroidery scribbled flowers of Xela were easy to identify, too. A few quetzals bought the outlines of a Xela neckband drawn in ballpoint on calico (I embroidered them by hand, my work too finicking in finish). Then, after weeks of indiscriminate dazzle on buses, I began to ascribe to their locations all the other counterpoint stripes, chevrons, rhomboids, birds big and little.

Huipiles, or *po't* – the Mayan names – I love more than the arum lilies of the fields. Because women toil at them, even if they don't so often spin any more. And Solomon in all his glory must have been arrayed in one of these.

A *huipile* is a rectangle of cloth seamed together from two or three narrow panels, woven on that ancient device, a backstrap loom. Long warp threads are tied at one end to the head bar, secured to a branch or a trunk, the mother tree, by a cord. (Everybody understands its connection with an umbilical cord.) A hook or roofbeam holds the cord where there is no tree. At the other end, a second bar splays the warp in proper order, and a strap around the waist, or hips, holds that bar. A weaver sits or kneels on her mat, itself woven of leaves, and tenses her warp — the north-south long threads — by leaning back, pulling them taut. She bends forward to relax the warp enough to slip through her weft — the shorter east-west threads. A small tunnel for the weft pulses open and shut in the warp between each tension and relaxation, between each turn of the shed sticks that elevates selected warps.

That vacancy is the heart of the Mayan loom. The rhythm of the weaving pulses like a strong, slow heart, and the body of the cloth is fed with the weft threads. (Marcador brocades are lightly picked through the warps and the beat not so strong.)

The heart beats all daylight hours not needed for domestic tasks, until the strips are complete. It can take months in a life of so many tasks. Then the strips are seamed together first into a great rectangle, then again under the arms into a simple tunic, with a hole for the neck.

When new, even the lightest *huipiles* are heavier than industrial dungarees. Over the decades of their lifespan – as they are laundered in washhouses and rivers, frothed in El Gallo soap powder suds, pounded – they soften until they feel like towels remembered from childhood. The time it takes to make a true thing by hand is stored up within it. And released as slowly, more slowly, back into a life as the thing is used. The days of its making unwind again.

Everything that is Mayan has four corners. And four sides. And a centre, in which the trunk of the body and the world tree stands. Ever since the Maize God laid out the cosmos and set the stars and the planets turning like a spindle, with the sky as thread, the repeating patterns of humans have been woven along the warp of time. These patterns become comprehensible only when the loom tension is at last slackened. The cords are cut after the final selvedge is woven in.

Mayan reliefs and stelae of thirteen hundred years ago and more record *huipiles*, and their patterns. Early mornings at Palenque or Tikal, the oblique sun will outline a familiar sequence on a stone or stucco robe. The graven women have hair piled up and sculpted with ribbons and pompons, as women still wear it in Zunil. *Huipiles* are not unchanging, though. Those who can make can modify. They borrow novelty by eye: Dayglo pink and glitter acrylics and cabbage roses.

In Zunil, the *huipile* has ceded some of its power to a huge shawl thrown over all, and to narrow wrap-around skirts brocaded on the treadle-loom that figures repeats so neatly. I subsided on a step, among papery corn-cob shuckings, to sit at eye-level among the posies, grape bunches and loping cats woven on those skirts. Women define themselves not as Mayan, but as 'women of the skirt' – makers and appreciators and models all at once. Where the men were not masquerading, they wore the no-place factory-made shirts and jeans of the Americas from El Paso southwards. A few from a stubborn Mayan town wore the archaic short wool kilt and bare legs.

Close smells from the plaza of smoke and piss. On the paths up towards the highway, drunks lay where they fell. When the rain and dark came down, and the lock-up in the corner of the plaza filled, the cops seemed agitated beyond the strenuousness of celebration. The blue wool tassels on their nightsticks bounced as they sought their comrades in the crowds.

Panajachel, Atitlan.

None of the newspapers dared be candid, but *Prensa Libre*, bought from the plaza in Xela, admitted the size of the event in the town of Santiago Atitlan over the weekend. There had been plural narratives in every Xela bar. The massacre, *matanza*, sounded more like a revolt. This story was told several times: the new commander of the army base near Santiago used to drink for free in town; swaggering drunk, he bammed on the door of a woman he fancied. Neighbours grabbed him, he loosed a round, his base heard it and sent a patrol, or more, who shot a boy and freed the commander. Shot others, too. A 1000, or 3000, or 6000 (no agreement) people from Santiago Atitlan, alarmed on to the night streets by church bells, had walked a mile to the base – demanding the commander be handed over to the authorities, no more interference, no more disappearances (over twenty men of the town gone that year, 1,000 in a decade). They wanted to be able to work up on the slopes of the volcano above the town without fearing the military, and to move in their own streets by night. *Prensa Libre* reported that there had been a 'fusillade' at the base (as if the army weapons had been muskets). The surrounded soldiers had fired on the crowds. Eleven dead, or thirteen, the Atitecos guarding bodies left on the ground overnight, so these would not disappear. Two or five more surviving in Solola hospital.

Reckless buses, cockaded with fowls in baskets, were, are, all the transport in Guatemala, and suddenly there was a gasolina crisis and a dispute about fare increases, so no transport to Lake Atitlan for one day, then two, then not until after the funeral. Even then there was only a single vehicle, unsure of its route, its roof-rack dressed with passengers instead of chickens. Another gringo was inside, so American-tall that, standing, he had to curve his head into the aisle roof. He politely handed back change from the driver to the passengers, and attempted to sit over the aisle gap with a quarter of a buttock on each seat. Bill, an ex-chemist. He had followed the logic of chance, and a little surplus money, to Guatemala. He had just heard about the *matanza* and meant to search for eyewitnesses. He had to be back in Xela by the next night for the inauguration of his apartment and explained how its floor tiles had been laid on thick sand so that utility pipes could be inserted later. His Peace Corps friends would be present for the party (young men like him but with thin ties and short-sleeved shirts) and he thought that they might know more about what had happened at Santiago.

The resort of Panajachel by Lake Atitlan had emptied, its trade evaporated. Bill and I walked the parallel narrow roads of the town, which ended at the lake. They were deserted. No vendors, no weaves hung on their branch frames. A wind began to lift the soil, which was sandy towards the water. All ferries had been withdrawn from the lake, and there was no crossing to Santiago. Nobody would talk about putting out a boat.

The American owner of a desolate bar said the international press had been and gone long since by car from Guat City. He had not gone to the funerals, personally. Nobody from Panajachel had. He was not interested, personally. You live here, you don't get interested.

Under the jacaranda out back of the bar, a Quebecois, a chess-playing buddy of Bill, drank beer with his girl. She was in Latina clothes in the Madonna mode, but the bones of her face were off the stelae. She was a translator, she said, not through the university, self-taught: 'You want to eat, you keep quiet.' Rings flashed on the fingers and thumb of each hand. 'You keep quiet, but you don't have to believe.' Where she came from, whole families had gone. There had been soldiers on Panajachel's beach these last few days. But always there were soldiers on that beach, the helicopter went back and forth. Soldiers were given liquor. By the rich. Why? To enrage. On that she was very insistent.

Birds spluttered and squawked in the palms. Bill asked questions, including the name of 'the recording artist' being played. The conversation drifted into the hallucinatory, the normal mode in

Panajachel. Why did American X get his head cut off? Because he humiliated army men with karate. And the bookshop owner shot one night, though his wife was politely only grazed? Books second, cocaine first. The Quebecois enjoyed making the hand-as-pistol gesture. Boom-boom. He tied a Guatemalan scarf over his baldness. The girl was dissolving into drink and watching him. When he went to pay, she said: 'I been with him three times today.' But she was not looking at him, nor at me, but at the storm dropping down from the heights around the lake, shaking the trees. Lightning flashed silently within the mist.

Bill charmed a severe American dame who had been there twenty years into feeding him. Santiago was full of internal feuds, she said. Everybody let them get on with hating each other. The ferries were out because the army had commandeered vessels to ship men, young recruits, sometimes pressganged illegally, fourteen, fifteen years old. Bill and I sat late on the beach staring over each other's shoulders at the lights of villages, including Santiago, across the water. Soldiers doubled quietly to a landing stage, but no boat came in.

All night a north wind irritated the lake rim. Ferns and fronds swashed even in the courtyard of the hotel where Bill had negotiated a cheap room for us to share. He chose the bed under the window, its handwoven curtains rising in the wind. He was next to the unfitted door, which rattled, and he could not sleep. He did not say why he was angry.

Santiago Atitlan.

Bill had gone home to Xela on the only bus to move out, the underfloor of his apartment winning out over curiosity. There were fresh turquoise crosses, the Mayan green at the centre of the four-pointed universe, in the soil in Santiago cemetery. A van with a loudspeaker worked the steep streets, selling a not-quite new newspaper. Three colour pix of the funeral: the sepia stripes of the short trousers of the Tzutujil men of Santiago registering poorly.

Through the town, black polythene snapped at halfmast from poles, or was twisted around poles above doors, windows. A sombre feria across alleys. Down on the shore, a small boy flew a black plastic bag as a windsock kite. Mayan kites, which are huge paper and feather wheels, the headdresses of the gods, interpose in the sky between the living and the dead. A lift to the spirits.

Santiago was being claimed by the American evangelical churches. Each with some name of Zion: Bethel, Eben-Ezer, Nazareth, Capernaum. Each 'missionarising', as one of their personnel put it on a non-ferry boat half-way across the lake, 'the heathen Indians'. The idea of heathen-ness seemed peculiar, given that, since at least the 1730s, the Catholic church had discreetly accepted that Catholicism was practised hereabouts as a metaphor for Mayan habits. 'This violence would stop if they would only accept Jesus Christ as their personal saviour,' she said, and her face puckered. She picked at worry dolls on the band of her straw hat. 'I try to understand the way they live,' she said, unasked. 'Living in a hut may not be that awful. Not for them.' She was a Latter Day Saint — an Ultimas Dias — not one of Jehovah's Testigos, although they were there among the azure-painted breeze blocks. Some of the churches demanded that their converts give up *traje* as part of renouncing who they had been. Others just pointed out how hard it would be, when their home was proclaimed by their clothes, for men to sell their labour along the coast and in the cities.

Santiago's Catholic church had a sheet metal roof and electric bulbs round the door. The American in charge might have posed for posters for Buffalo Bill's Wild West Show. He said without any edge that the parishioners conducted their own affairs. 'Sometimes when the funeral's happening, they [local nuns] let me know who it was.' The newspaper with the colour photographs, being a city publication, had added automatic melodrama about Atitecos' affection for Maximon, the legless devil-saint. Legless, in every sense. He drank. Maximon's image lived in a brotherhood house and went about on holy days: he might be Judas, or Alvarado, or simply Ladino laxness in effigy. Children scooting in and out the parish office offered an introduction to him, for money. The morning landing of tourists was the town's cash flow – tips on the dock path, quetzal notes for the little one, more to photograph women with ten metres of scarlet braid coiled around their heads. But there had been no tourists for days.

I went and sat in the colonnade of the mayorial office, out of the sun and wind, opposite the market. It was not a special day for fine clothes as it had been at Zunil, and yet all the women and most men wore *traje*, handwoven in white and aquatic colours. Orchids and roses garlanded the necks of *huipiles*. Around the hems of men's trousers, a wide band was embroidered with birds. Many were handworked in an expensive French thread: the flamingo plumage and the tufts of owls were stitched in firmly, so that they did not catch on lake reeds as their wearers went about their work. The thread shops sold crib sheets of chromoliths of birds, like the frontisplates of old natural history books.

Women knelt among brassica leaves to buy and sell vegetables. They unknotted a corner of their stoles, extracted a Nivea tin, and took out of that not so much as a pound in notes that had been handled until they had returned to rags. Awnings dipped low over these transactions. Flies ricocheted. Through hammering and words in Spanish and the clicks of Tzutujil, a young woman sobbed under her mantle. She was hunched in the dust against a doorpost. Nobody paid attention.

According to journos lunching in a shack *comida*, there was an agreement among the Atitecos to march again at 4 pm to the army base and demand the permanent withdrawal of the military. The journos were a young bearded Englishman with a mike, stringing for Bush House and a grizzled American in a rainproof poncho. (Maybe we should go talk with his friends in the campesino movement, he said. If I was so interested in trees, did I know there had been peach orchards above the town until they had been mined by the army?) The third journo was a girl, just being The Girl. All three were up from El Salvador for the last pickings of the *matanza* – talking danger, also deciding whether to take the last possible boat over the lake or stay for the march. They did not want tortillas with their meal, they must have bread. Each explained what happened. So did the *comida* keeper. And her husband. No two accounts converged.

    I bought food and water in a shop. The family who ran it were different. A daughter minded the counter, dispensing stale spongecake and writing in a schoolbook. Then she and her brother mixed a great tub of coconut mush, while their mother read aloud from the newspapers. Father, wary, paced beside the entrance. Later, the tub was taken into the compound behind the offices, to feed the town defenders. The Catholic church's Buffalo Bill had said education, a little business, made radicals of schoolteachers and shopkeepers.

Police walked into the plaza centre with a few Atitecos, seniors.

This was the balance moment.

All the kerbs filled with women and children come to see what would happen, to look at each other's *huipiles*, and sell oranges to each other.

Nothing happened.

I wandered down to the shore and looked up at the high fields on the volcanoes, made out a twitch of fire. Why were so many people lining the jetty – where no further ferry was expected – silently looking down?

A coffin was manhandled down steps towards the water. All along my route that winter a coffin-maker's had been just another ordinary shop – between the suppliers of sharpeners for machetes and the treadle sewingmachine stockist. Always at least a dozen boxes waiting around the walls of businesses named 'Ultimate Rest' or 'Final Benediction'. Wood shavings curled on the floor. At funerals, they broadcast the 'Dead March' from *Saul*, the 'Hebrew Chorus' from *Nabucco*, and those who carried the coffins kept practiced step. At least fifteen caskets had been used in the last few days in Santiago and they still had a spare.

At the water's edge was the corpse of a man, floating face downwards. The stripes of his plain trousers – without birds or fake-Mayan glyphs – showed through the orange plastic bag in which he had been bundled. The watchers were calm. From time to time, bored children broke away and returned to tug their kites, or mind a cow. A woman drew her tzute-stole over her head and walked away. Otherwise, silence apart from a wrangle over the coffin. Since no one could be found to pay for it, it was hauled up the steps again.

I told the journos. The American said the orange bag made it 'bizarre, I mean, even for *Twin Peaks*'. They enquired at the mayor's office. The corpse was a fisherman who had drowned in the north wind that rattled the doors; he had only just been netted in. Cedar from volcanic forests made strong dug-out canoes, but they did not always outrun a north wind.

The mayor's office also said that a concord had been reached. The soldiers promised to withdraw from the base (although no one believed that they would). The journos dickered over hiring a canoe with an outboard. They stood a little distance from the orange sack in the water and were stared at steadily. On the jetty's other side, a girl took down a bowl from her head, mixed a solution of El Gallo in it, and pounded a *huipile* on a rock.

I stuck around the lake, sat on doorsteps in Santiago, listened to the looms inside. (A treadle clacks, whereas a backstrap has a bass tump.) I watched the smoothing water and the volcano slopes over the edges of my embroidery.

When I finally returned to Pana, I was nauseous, and it took days to pass.

Pana had a bar called The Circus, on its walls signed photographs of artistes; in a concrete hangar claiming to be Central America's largest permanent Big Top, the trapeze hung over dusty tables.

There were deserted restaurants, and a teashop whose manageress, wearing gloves and beret, walked two big dogs on leashes. A woman of the skirt came to the teashop's side door to have a pail filled with peelings for her chickens. A man in faded red from Solola town up the hill stood outside and begged food. The boss told the manageress she might give him 'a portion of bread'. She handed him a paper-wrapped roll.

In the empty street, the bar-owner-who-hadn't-been-interested, personally, pulled up a chair outside a café. He was with the chef at the Los Amigos restaurant, who was teaching the art of marination to Alfredo, from the city.

They hailed foreign women passing down the main street, 'Ola, sweetheart' – and rated them when they were out of hearing. 'All whores.' They agreed that if the gasolina troubles lasted, they could charge $20 for a ride out of town, $40 anybody wanted Guat City. The quetzal rate to the dollar was down. A black *Norteamericano*, who introduced himself as an anthropologist, asked if that guy in the antiques trade still had good jade?

'Sure. Last time I saw him, he got phone call, said his brother shot. Boom-boom. What you here for?'

'Holiday. Lotsa girls.'

A gringo with long centre-parted hair gestured at the Video Cinema adjacent. It had hand-written schedules for six or seven films a day – none actually showing. 'Same old films,' he said of a running order *El Norte, Baghdad Café, Paris, Texas*. 'When they gonna get *Biker Chicks from Zombietown*? These chicks have a club called The Cycle Sluts.'

Soda water didn't ease the nausea, nor did rest in a hammock. The wind rose again each night, poking broken ribs of palm through the gap under the door. I began to embroider a new piece of unbleached calico, bought in Xela, inked with grapes on a vine and the word 'Felicidades'. That helped.

There was hardly a road around the north side of the lake. To get from Pana to Santiago by land was almost a day on foot, half of it on one of those foot-wide paths along the top of a cliff, with boulder stairs and washouts. It had probably been a path for 1,500 years. Fat corncobs hung from high stems growing so close to the cliff edge there was sometimes almost no path left. Along wild stretches, grass grew in a tough arc above the bent heads of those who used the path as a haulage route. It blinded and choked them with its seeds. Twice it sent me almost over the edge, and I had no pack. The second time I kept only one knee on the path, which had crumbled away to six inches, and pulled myself back up by clutching stalks. Ten minutes further on, small barefoot boys – each with a heavy bag on a tumpline around his forehead – passed at a fast pace. The biggest was old enough to sweat. His T-shirt was black. As they went out of sight, he turned and waved. When I reached that point, the path was gone, just a slither of loose stone.

From the path you could *see* waterside retreats. But they were reachable only by speedboat. Some were finished, some under construction. There was more glass in a single picture window than in all of the villages on the way. A hose rainbowed over a garden. A mausoleum-like stone building stood on a promontory. Motor launches arabesqued on the lake.

Where the path dropped to cross valley bottoms, I met farmers and banana pickers. Just before it became a dirt road through coffee plantations, it detoured by a stream through an orange grove. Waterfalls bobbed with fallen oranges. Flocks of black and lemon butterflies flapped over the fruit.

A man who sold *refrescos* from a shack said he knew an hour ago a *gringa* was coming. He said I made poor time for someone with long legs and boots.

We were at 6,000 feet or more.

'You carry nothing.'

White polythene flags had joined the black in Santiago, inscribed with ballpoint slogans: 'Where is the peace?' None of the Atiteco bands had witnessed any ship-out of soldiers, but neither was the army loping insolently around town as before. The Mayor proposed to ask for human rights observers to monitor the military departure – 'for ever'. Inside the church, the nuns led prayers for peace. An aggrieved assembly in the plaza turned out to be the announcement of a lottery. The shopkeeper's wife ran out to spend quetzals on the weekly *Extra* – full as usual of mortuary photographs of the unidentified dead. Pages of slab shots. She was disappointed that no victim of the local *violencia* had made it to the magazine and said perhaps they would next week. In all the Spanish songs I heard from above the Rio Grande to Santiago that winter, the most frequent word had been not *amor*, love, but *corazon*, heart.

Up in Solola, where the road rose from Lake Atitlan, it was the season for burning the devil. Men and women flickered like flames themselves in their woven *traje*, narrow-striped scarlet and orange and pink. Sudden fires of cardboard and trash blazed up outside doors, and left foul-smelling ash.

Chichicastenango: The sole bus out of Xela to Chichi had had to slow over the *tumolos*, bumps in the road that controlled transport (when there had been transport). It passed a Zona Militaria, which gave passengers time to admire a masterpiece of folk art. The zone's gatehouse was a huge concrete sculpture, a DPM-patterned helmet atop a pair of black boots with fashionably butch white paracord lacings. It was only slightly a joke. Real weapons pointed from the slit in the helmet. Every man in the bus pulled out the cross on a chain or cord around his neck, and clamped it between his teeth until the base was well past.

Chichi, 'Guatemala's Mecca de Turismo' (the placards read) was without tourists, too. Its Hotel Santo Tomas, once a monastery, had 50 rooms, a swimming pool, two fountained courts, with cockatoos, macaws and parrots on stands and swings. A tall cut tree desiccated in the inner court, hung with diamonds wound of yarn, 'eyes of God', open on the cardinal points of the worldscape. The tree was not a Yule fir but the ceiba that fruited with everything the earth needed: a Mayan-Christian co-production for Christmas. I dined alone in the hall set with cutlery for 100. The solitary, grave waiter wore a jacket properly belonging to the *cofradia* religious brotherhoods of the town – frieze wool, embroidered with sunwhirls. His leather sandals creaked as he fetched food. It felt impertinent to ask for coffee. (I would never have stayed there if the desk clerk had not been in the street and proposed a cheap rate as I passed.)

A *National Geographic* team was staying at the other uniformed establishment, the Mayan Palace, making a film about 'the thrilling world of the Ancient Maya'. They griped over lunch about the magazine's policy of no upgrades for film crews to business-class on short-duration flights. They had grievances over baggage allowance. The Palace dining room overlooked the pastel sepulchres of the *cemetario*. My window at the back of the Santo Tomas let in the sunrise over thin woods: through it I could see very early every day an open truck arriving, packed with women in *huipiles* brocaded with roses, *tzutes* over their faces to capture their warm breath in the cold air. Their colours blurred as they jumped down from the truck.

The church of Santo Tomas was on one side of Chichi's Mayan sacred square. The steps to its door were themselves sacred, rising in a ragged half-circle, with a stone for offerings at the apex. All day on the steps censers were swung – perforated tin KLIM and Carnation milk cans, with string handles, filled with copal. On stone floors inside, many candles, patterns of petals, libations of alcohol. Flames whispered. Wardens scraped at the wax of burnt-out offerings. After two days in the porch, I was so fumigated with copal that the hotel's scalding water did not wash it away. I went there to embroider, stemstitching the grapes in circles; as I worked, I admired over the edges of my calico the Chichi huipiles with designs like Victorian carpets.

It was a blessed week anyway: the festival of the Virgin of Guadalupe, madonna of the Americas, the dark-skinned Mary standing on a horned moon. Her image had been there all the way south, the Virgin wrapped not in the blue robe of Europe but in a parrot-green mantle ordered with stars, girdled in splendour, and wreathed in the roses she had made bloom out of season. *Nuestra Senora de Guadelupe* was so clearly the divine form of the women of the skirt that it seemed wrong that she had come to represent Latinness, (that is, re-exported Spanishness) to Hispanics north of the US border. She belonged to the Aztecs as the pregnant 'little mother' goddess Tonantzin and as the goddess Coatlicue, 'Our Lady of the Serpent Skirt', earth mother of all living things. She belonged to the Mayans who came before and stayed after, because the crescent she stood on linked her to Ixchel, wife to the Mayan moon god, who had taught women to weave with a spider as exemplar.

In Mayan highland Guatemala, when a women grows old she weaves her burial costume. The rest of her clothes, and the sticks of her backstrap loom, lie in the coffin with her. In Coban, if there are too many clothes, they are granted separate burial.

For Nuestra Senora, tableaux of small children, dressed as lilies or winged as angels, stood on the steps of El Calvario, the other pre-Christian foundation on the far side of the plaza. Vases of gladioli toppled in the evening wind. The children had mobile eyes but otherwise kept still. They were saving their excitement for a small fair – booths of painted canvas, pitched in streets around the plaza.

A Swiss-Italian architect, Pietro, arrived in the courts of Hotel Santo Tomas – a dandy planning to raise money for a reservation for endangered parrots. The green parakeet said 'una tortilla' for him, but not for me. The white cockatoo crested up for me but not for him.

In the midday sun, which was almost warm, the staff braided wreaths of pine. On a table in my room they set a clay nativity in a grass shelter shaped like the Mayan centre-doored, through-drafted building. I added a beautiful crowd of figures pinched of clay and mantled in scraps, bought from peddlers in Chiapas. The cold grew sharper early and late, so I bought wood for my fireplace. The paper and twigs flamed briefly, but the logs, no matter how propped and angled, would not catch. I had to hide even my head under the Momostenango blanket to heat up enough for sleep. Pietro bought for warmth a jacket patched of weavings from a dozen villages around: their unfaded anilines were harsh. Because they now had two residents, the staff lit fires in the dining room, and we returned to it after the Virgin's festival fireworks, our woven layers scented with gunpowder, woodsmoke and copal. We sat far apart to inhabit more of the space. Sparks cracked out.

The weekly market at Chichi followed Braudelian principles – surplus, abundance, piled high. It was descended from the pre-Columbian mercantile principles that had so impressed the Spanish, who wrote that the markets of this new world were bigger, and more stocked with cloth, than any in Renaissance Europe. That week, though, the market and the fair were missing vendors because of the strike and post-Atitlan nerves, and few trucks got through. A party of Germans and Americans did alight from a coach, and their voices cut across the parakeet as they ate in our hotel dining room. Then they were gone. Pietro left with them, zippered into his blouson, ready to amaze Geneva.

And then I was alone again.

The fires were let to go out.

Each day the hotel owner tugged his big dogs on leads past the dry swimming pool. The coach had brought newspapers, with editorials about the moderation of the compromise at Santiago, where the army had not yet budged. The number one story was the unusually cold pre-Christmas weather in Guatemala City.

It was hard to walk out of Chichi by road. Boy soldiers at the post on the way to the cemeterio – their rifles on handwoven slings – would not permit it. But off the road there were those economical paths between orchards. Maize sheltered daisies and squashes on vines. I stood aside in them to let by a woman – bent double under bundles of striped cloth and leading a cow to market. A file of soldiers pushing bicycles forded a stream, carrying the bikes across high and dry. On slight elevations there were blackened patches, empty bottles, copal ash. When I struck a road again, I was offered a lift in a pick-up truck by girls turbanned green, like a flock of parrots. It was such an excitement to join them I missed the turn and had to be dropped off in an unexcavated but known Mayan ruin. Its ball-court was discernible. Beans and corn grew between its platforms. I could see the burnt circles of contemporary *brujos*, sorcerers, on its stone steps.

A party of Italians – three family men, pipe-smokers, and a strong young woman – reached the hotel, demanding coffee and pastries. They asked me to dinner, but would not speak much about the development project they worked on. Their patroness joined us. Several languages were not quite being spoken, so I did not catch if she was the minister's wife or sister or sister-in-law: Madame Elvira. Under hard-cut bleached hair, she too had a face from the stelae. Tight trousers, frilly blouse. A waistcoat of dyed fur. She travelled with a plain girl as foil to answer questions. Her manner solicited half-sexual compliments. She ordered only fruit for dinner, then ate more of the meal than the rest of us from the men's plates. She turned each question towards sex.

The woman of the Italian party wrapped her rough Guat jacket about her and would not be put off. How many active volcanoes? Did the land use much fertiliser? Did all the villages have different costumes?

Madame Elvira fielded her fact-maid to answer these. The fact-maid was somehow despised for having the answers.

Half a tree burnt in the grate. Five waiters attended in sunburst jackets, their heads dignified with embroidered cloths.

Madame picked up on a question about traditional steam baths: 'No, no, never men and women together, Indians don't like that kind of fun.' She ate a big forkful of chicken and dabbed her mouth with a napkin. 'No, there is no traditional use of drugs here, but we have them. It is all the Colombians' fault. The indigenes are poor, but, you know, very happy. Their lives are full of beauty and flowers, we are proud the tourists come so far to see them, we will have the children put on a show for you, what a pity the swimming pool is finished for the season now, we could have gone for a swim. If you buy anything be careful for the insects, the indigenes are not clean. For myself, I do not like the Indian clothes. Miguel will help you with your computer. Just tell these people what you want. We are doing all we can to help them. You will see how they smile at you.'

The Italians worked hard at gallantry but Elvira retired early and her fact-maid followed. The Italians ordered complicated drinks. I sat in front of the fire as it burnt down to embers, satin-stitching the word 'Felicidades'.

Next morning was the first day of a fiesta. A *cofradia*, a religious guild dressed as the waiters were, but with silver staffs, carried three twenty-foot constructions – of feathers, mirrors and flowers – up the strange stairs, and set them out in the church. They might have been the world tree that provided all. Or the head-dresses of the gods. In the street just by the church, where the fair was pitched, there were children on a simple big wheel, swung round by arm-power alone. I could smell chips frying, cut wafer thin from waxy potatoes. A festival licenses a waste of fat.

Madame Elvira and her bodyguards drove away from the hotel in a dark-windowed car.

The final count in Santiago, said the paper when I left Guatemala City, was seventeen dead.

Adam Foulds

The Broken Word

<u>Chapter 1: What Was Happening</u>

Compact glare of a match flame in daylight

and the waiter's dark hand still
as an ornament, the flame an upright leaf
tending to Jenkins as he sucked his cigarette alight,
because the train had slowed.
He wished it wouldn't slow, not
among the lion-coloured slums
with their cattery stink.
He could see them posting themselves,
third class, into the train windows or dropping
carefully onto wide, unfeeling feet.

The waiter waved out the flame.
Can I get you a drink, sir?
Sun's over the yard arm.

The waiter stood in the cylinder

of his white shift, understanding
or not. The train bucked,
gathering speed. He levelled himself
naturally as a glass of water.

Jenkins blew smoke towards him.

Also there is an Englishman, English boy,
sir, on the train with ... other people.
Really? Who?
I don't know name, sir.
Well, tell him to come and see me,
and the answer is yes, bring me a drink.

*

The carriage dark with bodies.
Bright smells of opened fruit.
He asked questions and had
one old man talking because
he loved the plush impacts
of their consonants, the glimmer
of teeth, and had missed the sound
of thoughts fetched and weighed
and slowly spoken, ideas
that had formed slowly, in the sun,
a million miles from the bark
and whine and snivel
and brag of school.
It soothed him. The noble cheekbones soothed him.

The old man looked like Joseph

from his own farm
who always had something
small and alive to show.

He spoke of his son in the city,
the difficult life, and ambition.

Then a cough, a touch on his shoulder.

Excuse me, sir. Mr Jenkins invites you
to go to him, please.

              *

Tables. Empty Seats. Napery.
The proper way to sit.

This Jenkins, half-remembered, had a tweed moustache:
threads of ginger brown and white

I assume you don't smoke yet

and hair so thin and waxed,
fastidiously flat,
it looked like a lick of paint.

You haven't been back long.
Jenkins observed the boy's white skin
as though the observation were cunning.

I flew in this morning.
And school?

Is finished. I go up to university in autumn.
Jenkins, who had not been, did not ask which one.
*Final summer. You might have stayed in England,
you know. It might have been better.*
Tom said nothing, then: *I wanted to come back.*

Jenkins held his cigarette down
into the ashtray until it was out,
the last smoke crawling up his hand, into his sleeve.

*I presume your father has written to you
about the situation.*

Tom, trying to pull his eyes politely
back from the view to Jenkins:
He mentioned it.

It's bad enough, Jenkins leaned forward
sending quiet words out one by one
like bees from the gap of their hive,
*that you should not be in there
talking with them.*

Tom blinked, fingertips on table edge.
But I've always …

*Oh, we've all always but things are different.
The oathing has been going on
round your father's estate.*

Oathing?
*The ceremonies, the pledges:
join or your throat cut.*

*Or worse. Not far from here
two wouldn't.
Cut to bits, buried, dug up,
and then others forced to eat bits,
keep them in line. Of course
one broke down and spilled it.*

Jenkins regarded Tom, the boy's
fingertips still on the table edge,
mouth slightly open, blushing
with fear, the fine and healthy fear
that might save him.

*

Jenkins was met by Fuller
who led him to the car under trees already black,
the first stars prickling in their branches,
the two men walking, not talking.

Then, in the car, Fuller:
*We've picked up two more.
Oh, yes?
Yes. Chaps got a bit worked up,
actually, sort of let them
have it somewhat.*

*

Jenkins decided as soon as he saw
what a hash they'd made

of their faces, heard
their soft noises, lying there.

Mr Prior

the youngest there, smoking from
a flutter of fingertips, legs crossed,

      take these gentlemen
outside and end their suffering, would you.

Prior looked up. No one else looked.
When he had them up on their feet
and out of there, briefly,
at each other, they looked.

He made them walk in front.
Seeing their hands tied
in the smalls of their backs
his brain was smitten with a thought,
over complicated, strictly meaningless,
like a fever thought:
the captive's captive hands
and he the captor, three boxes: outermost he,
innermost, their hands, their bodies'
own prisoners.
It made no sense.

Stepping with his dusty brogues
into the weak backs of their knees
he made them kneel
and to do it quicker than he could think
shot them   one   two

each opened head falling away
from his hand.

When Jenkins came out he looked up
and knew that there was more to do:
he'd have to clean
with bucket and sponge
each wet red gust
from the station wall.

    *

Home. The door swings inward.
His father – not mother,
or servant, or sister –
his father, small eyes wet with joy,
it seemed, and then the shock
of the unaccustomed points
of his face against Tom's
for a second-long embrace,
then backing away, bowing,
Come in, come in.

Sipping the fragrant blue acid
of a gin and tonic
he watched the room deflate
behind his talking father.
Distended with imagining
when he came in
it became ordinary, actual, too quickly
while his father spoke too quickly
of cousins, small matters, prices.

His sister entered
carrying one of the cats.
She poured it out
onto heavy front paws
and an inconvenienced trot
to hold her brother lightly
by the shoulders and kiss –
mouth screwed up, the soft collision
of her cheekbone against his.

How are you, Kate?
Mm, she said, holding his gaze.
Where's mum? She hiding?
She's out, Kate answered, *out in the fields.*
Mum is? His father crossed his legs.
Yes. Kate held his gaze.
I've bought a little telescope,
his father said, *for the stars. Like to see?*
Defo. In a minute. I must ... refresh.
Right-oh.

A servant closed the door behind him; receded.
Tom stood a moment, half out
of focus with fatigue, and confused.
He walked towards the bathroom
and, passing, glanced into his father's study.
Books were piled; so now his father read.
He stepped in, heard his own voice,
as another cat, out of nowhere,
suddenly went.
He picked one up. Tennyson:
an old school prize.
Desk drawers were open.

And there was the new telescope
on its three legs, staring at the floor.
What was happening?
This, and the train. And there
was that old daub
in its place on the wall,
an eighteenth-century family thing,
a hunting scene,
its arrested motion like stopped clockwork
which had bothered him as a child,
birds stuck in a cream cheese sky,
drab trees, reeds, grey water, curve
of a dog, the hunter trudging home
with his heavy bag.

Chapter 2: Dinner (1)

Frank was dead and he was very tired.

Frank was dead, dishevelled in his chair,
one ear falling away,
nose tip and lower lip gone,
dress shirt dyed plum.

Even through the thumps and flashes
of his own attack Charles had heard
with peculiarly greater concern
the *chit chit* of panga blades
into Frank's back
before the servants had retreated.

Frank was dead and Charles was exhausted.

He'd crawled up all the stairs,
the slow, successive risers:
gripping their tops,
pushing them down,
the last few almost too tall to scale,
to get to the shotgun under the bed.

It felt like his fringe kept coming loose
but it was wide drips of blood
that fell everywhere. His hands
were syrupy with it,
also the two pieces of gun
that wouldn't shut together.
That catch ... he couldn't:
it needed a fingertip that was gone.

He had a terrible headache.
Its massive pulse seemed outside
of him, one of them,
shaking the room.
Also the world had strangely blued,
with a wizening rim.

He swivelled in his leakage
and lay forwards
holding the two parts together
in a straight line towards the door.

Chapter 3: Dinner (2)

Kate in the bath before dinner.
Warm, soap-clouded water. Melodious drips.
Hair swaying heavily on her shoulders.

She sat up to look at her teeth
in the shaving mirror.
Two fingers in each side of her mouth,
lips jacked out and apart
to check for yellowness
of secret smoking.
She looked closely,
gasping and swallowing,
breathing through her nose, and saw
the smooth bevelled gums
flowing over the root of each tooth,
odd transparencies in the front teeth –
a sort of grain, near the bottom,
the colour of water –
the thick tongue that wouldn't lie still
behind its wall of teeth,
heavy and lifting, the edges curling,
dark blue veins and ugly strings beneath,
and, burning now with strain,
a link of skin between upper lip and gum
tight as a guy rope.
She dropped the lips back,
licked around, hummed
with everything back in place,
dabbled her finger ends in the bath.

*

A senior houseboy served the soup.
They skimmed their spoons correctly,
without noise, not touching china.

Leakey began again.
I should like to do it tomorrow,
if we can get them all together.

If you really think it's necessary.

It's a pointless risk if we don't.
Tom's mother was reasonable.

It is necessary, confirmed Jenkins.

Even if they haven't oathed themselves?

Done what? Kate asked.

Don't you ever read the papers?

Oathed themselves, Leakey repeated.

Tom looked at his large, calm, convincing head,
the gold cross perched slant on his collar bone.
But a man who spoke Kikuyu
better than English, was almost one of them.
Then some of them were Christian too,
Tom reminded himself, the loyalists,
but not all of them. It was complicated.

Leakey set down his spoon before speaking,
an authority.

They swear freedom or death, an oath
that binds them together

to do whatever is decided.

*Or death? So if they break it
they'll be killed*, Tom reasoned.

*Ah but the oath isn't properly binding,
just poor witchcraft.
These ceremonies can't be at night, for one thing.*

Jenkins caught Tom looking at him.
It's a precaution, he said.

And what's in your ceremony?
Kate wanted to know.

*Well, not all that they do.
We won't be sacrificing a goat
and drinking its blood, for instance.*

They do that?

Ceremony leaves them insane.
Jenkins tore his roll. *Degenerates.
They'll do anything. They drink
each other's blood as well, tell them*

Sometimes, Leakey confirmed.
*Incisions in the upper arms.
I don't think it's common.
They tell their god Ngai
to fight for them,
that he will be humiliated if they lose.*
His God invulnerable.

The two bars of gold,
dropped inside his shirt.
Leakey caught Tom's eye, smiled.
Have you ever drunk goats' blood?
You have to do it quickly
otherwise you're chewing down the clots.
Awful. Like ... melting gristle.

Maasai drink cows' blood, Tom pointed out.

We drink milk, Kate said.

Meaning what? her mother objected.

It's done under banana leaves,
my ceremony, which theirs always are.
And facing Ngai.
He dwells on Mount Kenya.
There's a special stone: the kisotho stone.

And blood pudding. And blood sausage.

Katy, do stop.

And Major Bloodnok.

Katy smirked with her father.

Leakey, swallowing soup,
eyelids lowered, submitted to smile.

Nurse, the screens!
Jenkins called to the servant by the door

who wavered forwards, was waved back.

So, Leakey spoke again,
how many are on your land?

Jenkins: *I hasarded a hundred,
plus household staff.*

I don't think we need worry about them.

Jenkins laughed, dabbing up soup.
I would start with them.

Tom's mother corrected.
It's a little less, nearer eighty.

And I hope you all know how to shoot.

Tom said, *I read this area was loyalist.*

Oh well then no doubt it's perfectly safe.
His father, loud and satirical.

What? Tom breathless, his face heating,
fed up of his father's snaps and ellipses.
Well, looking at his mother for support,
finding her face and Kate's
shut against the moment.
Well, isn't it?

But his father, head bent,
buttering three sides of a walnut-sized
tuft of bread, said nothing.

Jenkins answered.
Oh, it is. We've been recruiting
for the Home Guard.
Military job, really,
but the Police Reserve, we've done
all sorts lately.
It hasn't been ... entirely quiet.
And if they really turn...

Chapter 4: Facing Ngai

Mid-morning after rain.
Mountains flowing rapidly under clouds.
The valley paths a freshened red
with yellow puddles, glittering weeds.

Tom walked between the lines
of coffee for half a mile,
knocking fragments
of water on to his sleeves −
little bubble lenses
that amplified the weave
then broke, darkening in.
He walked to within earshot
and no further.

A surprisingly dull sound of ceremony,
one voice then many voices,
one voice then many voices,
that recalled school chapel
although probably they were spared hymns.

Tom remembered the hymns,
the light, weakly coloured by the windows,
falling on the boys opposite,
standing, opening their mouths;
and the hymn books,
the recurrent pages greyish,
worn hollow like flagstones
with pressure of thumbs, over years,
years of terms, the books staying always
on their dark shelves in the pews.
The days he wanted to stay
all day alone in the pretty, scholarly chapel.

And then over the voices,
another sound.
Faintly, from behind the house,
Kate practising with a pistol,
its faint, dry thwacks
a fly butting against a window pane.

Adam Foulds lives in South London. He has recently completed a novel, *The Truth About These Strange Times*.

Nicholas Murray

'It's Sybille'

1 June 2000: Chelsea

Even London, even the King's Road, looks beautiful on a June day such as this and it is nearly six in the evening as I turn off into a small street that runs down to the Chelsea Embankment. I am nervous. Not sure what I am about to encounter. This is why I have arrived so early, to avoid any practical glitches – unpunctuality, failure to find the house. I walk up and down the street, identify the house, a small, undistinguished entrance that I manage to walk past three times before I notice it. Am I being watched? Has someone phoned the police to alert them to a suspicious character casing the joint? I look at my watch and see that the second hand is sweeping towards six. I press the bell.

There is a long silence and I start to debate whether I should press it again. I raise my hand just as a sound reaches me of a bolt being drawn back, a mortise lock being turned, then another. I know what this reminds me of. Ten years as a Labour Party activist in Bermondsey in the Tatchell era, knocking on doors on embattled estates where elderly women live in a permanent state of siege, buttressed by locks and bolts and spyholes. But this is Chelsea and the woman on the other side of this door is one of the most interesting and distinctive writers of her epoch.

The door eventually opens and a small, frail, slightly bent woman peeps around its edge.

'Do come in, Mr Murray.'

I am writing a biography of Aldous Huxley with whom Sybille Bedford lived in the south of France and whose official life she wrote 30 years earlier and whom, I shall soon learn, she admires with the passion of a near-idolater.

I am led through to a single room at the back which seems to combine the functions of sitting room and study and which is very dark on this brilliant June evening. The house appears divided into three flats or maisonettes and Sybille's has light coming in from only one source, a French window in the corner. She invites me to join her on a chaise longue then disappears into the kitchen to fetch some wine. I make my first sweeping examination. Her desk is at an angle in the corner near the window and is piled up with books and papers. A copy-stand obscures a manual typewriter. There is nothing as contemporary as a computer. Books are piled on tables and the surrounding bookshelves are full. Sybille returns with two wine glasses and pours out a light wine of Alsace which she informs me is just right for this occasion and time of day. It is clear that she is not in perfect health, occasionally strains for breath, but her mind is as sparky as a knife on a whetstone. She explains that her latest book – the sheets of which are on that copy-stand – is costing her a great deal of effort. She describes it as a sort of memoir of the Twentieth Century which will say a little more about her relationship with the Huxleys. This will be *Quicksands*, published eventually in 2005 without the subtitle she now gives me: *Memoirs of a Survivor*.

I am struck at first by her manner of speech – very rapid, staccato, sharp, still with an unmistakable but very subdued German accent after all these years. I soon realise that the way she speaks is the way that the English intellectual élites spoke, élites among which she has always lived. Think of a crackly recording of Noel Coward's *Private Lives*. In the first few decades of the Twentieth Century, when the Murrays were pounding out songs around the piano in a poor street in Bootle, the upper-middle-class intelligentsia talked like this in Bloomsbury and on the lawns at Garsington, at villas in the south of France or on the Tuscan coast. She is a living link with that milieu. But she is also – and I thank her for this – a roving ambassador of civilised hedonism. I am instantly charmed in spite of an occasionally taut and disapproving *hauteur*, a sort of peremptory bridling at certain questions which the demands of modern biography require that I put to her.

She begins by talking very freely, recapitulating her view of the Huxleys and her continuing admiration for them and deploring recent books like David King Dunaway's *Huxley in Hollywood* and *The Hidden Huxley* (she thinks the latter tendentious in trying to make Huxley look politically suspect, a view I share while at the same time admiring the scrupulous scholarship of its editor, David Bradshaw).

She is concerned about recent reports of a sensationalist book on Huxley's beautiful Belgian wife, Maria Nys, written by a Belgian journalist Stan Lauryssens. Some months later I meet Stan for a beer in the Grand Place in Brussels and feel rather traitorous, especially as I like him and appreciate his kindness at handing over to me a copy of Huxley's FBI file for which he no longer has any use. His book, which apparently sensationalised Maria's lesbian activities, has not been translated into English and Stan is anyway now doing very well with his new Belgian crime thrillers. I was in Brussels consulting the Huxley-Nys archive at the Royal Library – the most scandalously ill-curated manuscript collection in the world.

Sybille needed little prompting (although she would later admit that she had indeed been wary because she had absolutely no idea who I was). When I gave her a copy on arrival of my little 1993 book on her friend Bruce Chatwin she demanded: 'Why wasn't I told about this?' But I think she never held back and was always frank. She says that Maria had written countless letters to her sister Suzanne (less personal and intimate than those to her other sister Jeanne) with the intention that they would provide a source for future biographical accounts. Towards the end of his life, Huxley had thought of writing some form of autobiography and had asked for the letters to be sent to him in Hollywood. They were destroyed by the fire that ravaged his Californian house in 1961. She concedes that up to this point 'Aldous was not very interested in his personal life'. This theme of lost papers is constant in our conversations.

She declares that she had known the Huxleys since she was seventeen in the south of France. Moreover: 'They got me out of France' when war broke out and got her to the USA. Unfortunately: 'I couldn't bear California.' The Huxleys were happy with California, she thinks, and didn't miss Europe: 'They didn't want to live the literary life.' I think she is putting a finger on their (and her) insider-outsider status that lingers still in the ambivalent response in England to Huxley. But on the other hand: 'They often thought they would come back for good.' He didn't want to be a centre of attention. Huxley was 'an extremely modest man'.

She goes on: 'Aldous's health was poor. He was very frail.' He suffered from bronchitis. And then, inevitably, we come on to his sexual adventures about which her own book back in 1972 was quite open, revealing the way Maria had helped him towards certain women: 'Aldous had the normal sensual appetites and he liked women. Maria saw this was a necessity for Aldous.' She told Sybille that women should never have the vanity to tie someone down, especially an artist – she gave the same advice to Suzanne, whose husband had open affairs including a long term relationship with someone who may actually have lived with them. 'It was part of being generous.' She confirms that Maria did indeed facilitate (the episode appears in Huxley's own fiction) but 'she did not encourage' these relationships which were very brief and superficial. She invited the women to dinner. 'She was feminine enough to see that they didn't try to claw Aldous away.' This would not have been wanted by him, however, because their relationship was so deep and important. 'They talked about it together. They were very free for their time.' But also: 'Aldous had an idea that sex could be very morbid and terrifying.' At the same time, however: 'He was very very easy and sensuous.' As Sybille puts it, sitting with me on the chaise longue, pausing from time to time as she gathers breath, he liked women who liked other women because he liked them himself. He had very many homosexual friends like Gerald Heard and would say, in the joking and pre-PC way people did in the 20s and 30s: 'The buggers are coming to lunch.' Frances Partridge, she adds, with an intimate wave of the hand as if I have just come from tea with her, still speaks of 'our bugger friends'. Once the Huxleys came to visit Sybille in Berlin and were taken to a raunchy night club. A man asked Aldous to dance and, in his gently obliging way, he allowed himself to be taken out on to the dance floor for a few steps.

But what about Stan's – and David King Dunaway's revelations? She concedes briskly: 'Maria had a penchant for women.' But certainly not, as has been alleged by Dunaway, for Garbo and Mercedes d'Acosta. They used to say of their friend Garbo: 'She's a poor neurotic.' Maria had 'one or two great attachments that lasted all her life'. One was 'an Italian woman' (identified below) but was the other Sybille herself? Almost certainly, but though this was the question everyone wanted me to ask about this triangle, and though I sidled up to it so many times, it bounced with a sharp ringing sound off the wall of steel with which Sybille had surrounded it.

'Aldous, after Maria's death, had affairs with some of the most spectacularly beautiful women in Hollywood, when married to Laura.' She is referring to Aldous's second wife, Laura Archera Huxley, 30 years his junior. 'Aldous would say: "It can be such a friendly and agreeable and sane thing."'

Changing the subject, taking another draught of that pleasant white wine, Sybille observes: the years after the war were 'very tough for the Huxleys' and Maria wore herself out as his driver, housekeeper, personal assistant. She read him books she didn't understand. (His eyesight was permanently impaired). But it is always Maria that Sybille wants to come back to. Lady Ottoline Morrell was the great love of Maria's life and the cause of her very early suicide attempt, swallowing ammonia, after which 'she could never eat properly'. This service of Aldous lasted all her life. 'She was entirely at the service of a highly strung man.' When Sybille saw Maria in Rome in the 1950s she seemed visibly tired out. Am I familiar, she asks, with the French word *usée*?

From the library vaults at the Harry Ransom Humanities Research Center in Austin, Texas, I have had brought to me, week after week, the correspondence between Mary Hutchinson, Maria, and Aldous. Their sexual partnership is to be the chief 'revelation' of my biography, and Sybille is of course well aware of it. This becomes a running theme in our conversations. Sometimes she regrets that I have mentioned it, at others she concedes that I could hardly not do so: 'It was a very strange, triangular thing. Mary was attracted by Maria and Aldous was attracted by Mary.' Mary allowed Aldous to pursue her 'only because it was a road to Maria'. 'It was the way that milieu lived.' Sybille adds that neither Maria nor herself (she had one fleeting, unsatisfactory encounter with Virginia Woolf) cared for the Bloomsbury set. This was because 'Maria had very high standards of conduct.' She disliked the bitchiness of Bloomsbury: 'It was an unkind world.' A key term in the Huxley milieu – I was to hear it again, repeatedly, when interviewing his son, Matthew, in Washington DC – was 'kindness'. The Huxleys, Sybille insists, had very high moral standards. They gave before they were asked; they were always helping people. They were 'saintly' in the way they treated people, including those who worked for them. 'I have never met anyone more moral.' 'Maria in a way was a lay saint.' She saw all the unkindness of Bloomsbury and 'the vanity of the Sitwells'.

Sybille's own biography makes much of the traumatic events of Huxley's youth, the death of his mother, the suicide of his brother, his temporary blindness. 'Aldous was very very warped by his early years. He couldn't face certain things. He couldn't, for example, face Maria's death.' She pauses for a moment. 'He was a very strange man.' But she defends him against the charge that he ran to America to escape the war, a charge still levelled by resentful English critics today. His stay in America during the war was not political escapism, she insists, though he had prophesied total destruction in the way people were later to do in relation to nuclear weapons. He thought London would be obliterated. I ask tentatively whether his wartime self-evacuation to the Mojave desert in California might have been an attempt to escape a reality he couldn't deal with (I have this constant sense that, for all his intelligent clear-sightedness, Huxley looked away from certain things) but she rejects this hypothesis out of hand.

About Laura, Huxley's second wife, Sybille is always trenchant and unsympathetic. So much so that one wonders if there is more to it than the fact that Laura was not Maria. When I met Laura, at the Hollywood home in Mulholland Highway she shared with Huxley and where he had died, she seemed very charming – if not particularly insightful about her husband: 'Most of Huxley's Hollywood friends thought she treated him abominably. She neglected him,' says Sybille abruptly. Consequently he had a fall from which he could have been protected. But at the same time, she concedes, they had 'many interests in common'. Sybille insists: 'Maria very much wanted Aldous not to be alone.' She therefore sought to anoint a succesor after her death. But there were various women she didn't want to get their hands on him (Peggy Kiskadden, for example, 'who would have married him like a shot'). The marriage to Laura (the Nys family wanted Rose, Maria's widowed youngest sister, to marry him but Maria didn't want that) was, Sybille claims, 'more or less engineered by Maria'. On one occasion at Sybille's house in Rome, while Aldous stayed with her on her roof garden, Maria took Laura to one side and told her to look after Aldous. 'It was a kind of consecration.'

Sybille pauses again, takes another deep breath. Although it is only ten past seven we have spoken rapidly and unceasingly and I can see that she is tired. She thanks me for noticing, and says: 'We should meet again.' She shows me out very quickly and I hear the locks and bolts starting to close behind me.

Four days later the phone rings.

She wants us to meet again and remembers that she had not mentioned someone.

'Bertrand Russell was very jealous of Aldous. Sexually jealous.'

'Everybody loved him – the shopkeepers, the petrol pump attendants. He was very shy.'

13 June 2000: Chelsea Old Church Street

I arrive for my second visit, this time a little earlier at 4 pm. Another fine June day hidden from us in this dark basement sitting room. No wine this time. Just a glass of orange juice.

I begin by asking about the period Sybille called in the last interview Huxley's 'conversion' around 1934. She says that this was not a sudden Pauline conversion but a gradual process resulting from Huxley's dissatisfaction with the 'deep cynicism and pessimism, the contempt for the stupidity and wickedness of mankind' that had dominated his writing and thinking hitherto (and which, one might add, had constituted the attraction of his writing for many). 'He suddenly felt he must develop. Negative cynicism was not enough.' Besides all this there was the fact that *Eyeless in Gaza* was not working. He did not know how it would end. He had a writing block. This was an aesthetic problem and also potentially a financial problem – what if he had no future earning his living as a writer? He also couldn't sleep properly. 'He was tired of being ill all the time.' He couldn't see properly, he 'held himself wrongly', something that would eventually propel him towards experimenting with the new Alexander technique.

But he also wanted to know what could be done, how one could 'help' and was therefore drawn towards pacifism. He had 'a very high level of intelligence and goodness' and 'he was a very complex man.' He was pre-occupied with spiritual and intellectual questions and so, in her judgment, eventually gave up being interested in the art of writing as such. He did not, however, take the course of trying to politicise his writing. When she says that Maria helped with the plots sometimes, I recall Isherwood's comment that the novel for Aldous was 'a necessary evil'.

Well into our second conversation, I notice that Sybille always talks of 'Aldous' and I reply with 'Huxley'. Is this a gap I can cross, a familiarity I can assume? I decide that it is not.

She returns to the theme of America: 'It is curious how untouched he was by America.' In the early 1950s he thought he might leave America and on a visit to the Lebanon thought he might settle there. It was peaceful and there was 'no politics' – a rare example, she concedes, of his failure to foresee. He loved Egypt but was disappointed by Greece.

'Aldous had terrible silences. He found it very difficult to communicate with people. They had to start conversations.' He found it an 'agony' to speak to people who served them in the house. Once he had to drive a maid called Camilla from Sanary-sur-Mer – where he was living – to Italy with Sybille. The maid confided in her: 'I don't think I can do this. What if I have to ask Signor to stop because I need to use the lavatory.' But when Sybille told him this he was amused and on the trip would ask every few miles if Camilla wanted to stop. 'He was very shy.'

Sybille, it is clear, has little respect for Aldous's father, Leonard Huxley. After my book appeared I received an unpleasant letter from Huxley's half-brother, Sir Andrew Huxley (who had much earlier declined to reply to a request from me for an interview) accusing me of denigrating his father by calling him 'a literary journalist'. Sybille went much further: 'Aldous was shattered by his mother's death and he despised his father and his frivolous re-marriage to a woman younger than Julian.' Leonard Huxley, she says, was an example of the triviality that recurred in the Huxleys in contrast to the general high seriousness that was enjoined on this very special intellectual dynasty. She adds that he couldn't keep his hands off the female pupils in his wife's school, Prior's Field, in Surrey. Had I included that in my book Sir Andrew's letter would have been even more vitriolic.

I ask Sybille if she can help me in identifying the whereabouts of various paintings and portraits, done by Huxley. I have seen only one, at the University of Southern California. Sybille wonders about this. No one in this story is very good at looking after things. She thinks many were left to Matthew, but when I ask him about this later he says he has only one or two in his garage and doesn't really know about the rest. There was one of Eddy Sackville-West and one of his pacifist-era friend Gerald Heard which was nicknamed by Aldous 'The Grand Inquisitor'. 'Eddy was very fond of Maria,' Sybille reflects.

I note how her judgments are always sharp and exact, as if previously pondered: 'Aldous was very naive about politics. He had friends everywhere except in the business world. He was a Victorian Englishman at home in the world.'

We return to the theme of America: 'He was amused by America.' He always used to ask Anita Loos if he was right about the details of American life in his novels. For example, until he spoke to her he was under the impression that an ice cream sundae was something you drank rather than ate with a spoon.

What did he think of the Sanary set, I ask? [Sanary-sur-Mer: where the Huxleys lived in a house called La Gorguette from April 1930, on and off, until February 1937, surrounded by artistic exiles such as Thomas Mann: a period memorialised by Sybille Bedford in her 1989 novel *Jigsaw*.] Cyril Connolly for example, who, from letters written by Huxley, seems to have been kept at arm's length: 'Aldous didn't want an ex-Balliol man on his doorstep, preventing him from getting on with his work.' He hated the excessive eating and drinking of the Connollys – they were seen as 'time-wasters'. 'Jeanie hated Maria.' The Huxleys were not bon viveurs in the Connolly fashion.

They disliked fancy restaurants. 'He was undernourished at home and at Eton. Maria smuggled butter and egg yolks into his mashed potato.' He was also very dependent on doctors and that, she suddenly suggests, might have been a factor in staying in America where he was involved with so many of them.

Whatever Huxley thought of American civilisation the rejection of his application for US citizenship 'really upset him'. After the hearing he was 'white as a sheet', saying: 'They won't have us here.' He went straight home to bed.

I ask why they left Italy. I say I have been to Forte dei Marmi on the Tuscan coast where the Huxleys lived in the 1920s and where D

H Lawrence came to visit, declaring that the wide, hard flat sand of the beach reminded him of Skegness. They left Italy, Sybille says, because of fascism. They chose Sanary to be near Lawrence.

'*Point Counter Point* enabled them to buy the house.' The famous hand-built red Bugatti driven by Maria in her cap and goggles around the bends of the Cote d'Azur was their one big extravagance bought with the *Point Counter Point* money. 'Aldous never looked at his bank accounts. He didn't want to think about money.' And a lot of it went towards helping others – Maria's family, or the education of his step brother and sister. 'Maria had a principle of giving without being asked.' She also could not understand figures.

The birth of Matthew so early was not a good thing. 'Having a child was bad for Maria's health.' She had many abortions, Sybille claims, illegally in Paris, and at the London Clinic. Birth control was available but 'Aldous was not very practical.' Once again we find ourselves circling back to the sexual dimension. Is it me, the vulgar biographer? Or is it Sybille, still wanting to say something, to be frank and fearless, but at the same time wanting to hold back? Nancy Cunard, for whom Aldous developed a hopeless passion, is mentioned but, according to Sybille, he was too 'effeminate' for Nancy who preferred more rugged masculinity.

The allegations about Maria's involvement in the Hollywood Lesbian circles, she keeps insisting, are absurd. They had a very rigorous regimen in America. They ate at seven and went to bed at ten and worked very hard. 'It was a very strenuous domestic life.' There was no opportunity, she implies, for the orgiastic.

Notwithstanding Sybille's original reaction in my first interview ('Oh, you're not going to dredge all that up, are you?') – I tell her that I have decided I must describe the Mary Hutchinson/Aldous/Maria triangle. The existence of the hard evidence in Texas makes it absurd not to, even slipshod. Sybille nods gently. 'You are quite right.' And, to dismiss my apprehensions she tells a story. Seeing my pen poised, she says: 'Don't write this down.'

The story is that Sybille, when writing her biography in the late 1960s, had lunch with Mary Hutchinson and apparently sounded her out about the relationship. The existence of the letters now in Texas was evidently alluded to. It was clear that Sybille had not been allowed to see these though she would know in essence what they contained. Mary then told her that, with their scandal-value, they would be a nice little nest egg for her grand-children.

Aware of the difficulties being made by the Hutchinson Estate for scholars at Texas (though they were subsequently to give me full permission to quote from them in my biography), I observed acidly: 'Collapse of moral high ground.' Sybille smiled in a sibylline fashion.

Once again, we had been talking for over an hour and Sybille was fading. I quickly said I should go and she rose and showed me out.

Just before she closed the door she announced:

'By the way, now it's Sybille, and Nicholas.'

As I walked back up to the King's Road I felt I had passed some sort of test but in what I couldn't be sure.

30 September 2000: Chelsea, Old Church Street

My third visit lasts about an hour and a half, and I am aware that it is both exhausting to her and, in some sense, a strain because it awakes memories of friends she has lost. As with the previous interviews her desire to speak fluently, yet at random, may result in a rather disjointed cascade of observations.

I begin by showing her some letters from D H Lawrence which imply that at the end of 1929 there was some discord between the Huxley couple. She says that Lawrence was quite wrong. They loved one another and depended on one another: 'Aldous was almost helpless without Maria.' He and Maria used 'sweetikins' as an endearment. But nonetheless, I ask, if Sybille and I are now frank about Maria's sexuality, why did she marry him? 'She had a sense of vocation before love.' The key was in her early life (and we have both seen the typewritten family memoir of Suzanne Nys, now in Brussels, which contains an anecdote about Maria's childhood where she compares herself to the loyal horse on the tow-path, pulling the barge). 'She was always devoting herself to someone.' Sometimes she was exhausted, suffered from migraines. *Usée.*

Like most readers of Sybille Bedford's memoirs I notice that I get very little later reminiscence. The glamour of Sanary, the lost Arcadia, predominates. So I am pleased when she tells a story about her last meeting with Aldous in London in the early 1960s. They dined at Rules in the Strand and then walked through the West End for two or three hours. Contrary to representations of his being half-blind and stumbling, it was Aldous who was steering her around obstacles.

He said to her at one point: 'Why is it that all the shop window dummies look like Jackie Kennedy?' Yet in spite of this warm walkabout by two old friends: 'We couldn't talk about Maria.'

Always, in these conversations, we circle back to Maria, the incomparable, the unforgotten. 'Maria amused and enchanted him.' They sometimes had the same lovers and she attracted attractive women to the house then Aldous took them over. 'Maria's loves were very much accepted by Aldous.' But he 'loathed male homosexuality'. He was always interested in other people's sexual behaviour and their visits to nightclubs. He would ask Sybille on her return from one of these: 'Have you been to the seventh circle of Hell?' He could also be 'extremely playful and light'. But at the same time there was about him – and Sybille says this to me unblushingly – 'a feeling of saintliness'. Nothing saintly, however, about Sybille's view of Laura to which we now return. Although, 'Aldous was very much in love with her', on her side there was 'huge ambition'. She was 'young and fresh...radiated health and great energy...he came to life again'. When their house in California burned down Aldous stepped in and removed two suits on a hanger and the manuscript of *Island*. 'Laura merely said it was "beautiful".'

I now make my last attempt to raise the question of Maria, Aldous, and Sybille herself. It is not easy and I am gauche. At one point I hesitate and mumble: 'What I am trying to say is...' She breaks in sharply: 'Yes, what *are* you trying to say?' What I am trying to say, and my next attempt I think succeeds, is that we describe, perhaps even celebrate the heterosexual loves of literary figures, so why were Maria's lesbian relationships not told, acknowledged, honoured as opposed to its being considered prurient to talk about them. I am sitting upright on a short chaise longue a few inches from this frail but intense woman whose gaze is clearly focused on me. She says nothing. I think I have hit home. She merely nods, no longer offering a challenge. There is a long silence – most uncharacteristic of our swift, dashing conversations to date – and then she starts to talk about her general distaste for 'Gay Pride' and the Human Rights Act's apparent outlawing of prejudicial behaviour towards homosexuals expressing physical affection in public. Her argument seems to be that greater stridency by gay people inevitably provokes a backlash ('queer-bashing' is the surprising phrase she uses).

This is my last attempt. Let others pursue this. Perhaps she has left us some account, some reminiscence, which will let the truth be known – if we are entitled to know it.

20 March 2002, 9.28 pm: a voice mail

'Nicholas, this is Sybille. I have just read your first chapter and I am deeply moved, brought to tears and grateful. I think it is wonderful: intelligent, excellent, humane. I couldn't have expected anything more wonderful about Aldous...I wish I could have been able to put it like that. I am deeply moved. It is so good, it needs to be said, it's beautifully done. I had no idea. I wish I could have put it that way...I am grateful and moved and happy and I hope the answering machine will tell you. Thank you. Good night.'

I put down the phone, speechless.

Earlier that day I dashed round with a copy of my biography after it was reviewed prematurely in *The Spectator* by Philip Hensher – who, we both think, has not read the book ('He is also quite wrong about Aldous'). A cold, blonde woman opens the door and unsmilingly takes the parcel from me. I retreat up Old Church Street which seems rather chillier than it did ten minutes before.

6 April 2002: a voice mail

Sybille leaves another answering message at my London number to say that she is getting on with the book (having reached the publication of *After Many A Summer*). She was 'very disillusioned' having read the *Financial Times* review. (Though the others have been excellent and only John Carey in the *Sunday Times* has trundled out his usual line on Huxley under the headline: 'The self-deluded and snobbish life of a gullible guru'. I share Sybille's disapproval – ('dreadful little man') – of Carey's monotonous line on Huxley which, in recent years, we have had a little too much of. The *FT* review was 'appalling about Aldous and not fair to you...it's very distressing.' She claims still to be reading the book 'with great fascination'. 'I think it's very good.' She seems to like the emphasis on 'the philosophical, the intellectual' matters. It has made her wonder what has happened to her letters to Maria and Maria's to her. Have they been destroyed in the fire or does Matthew have them?

8 April 2002: London

I ring Sybille back and we chat. She is clearly in two minds about the Mary Hutchinson material. She agrees with me that I had to make use of it – and even offers some more gossip. She says that sometimes she would let Mary Hutchinson into The Albany through a back door, covered up, in veils, at a time when she was 'officially' the mistress of Clive Bell. I can't quite decide whether she would have preferred it not to have emerged. She also says there was an element of 'pose' in it, as if the whole thing were no more than a game. She wonders whether she should set out some facts herself and leave them with her literary executors. I hope she has done this.

One thing we never discuss is the mysterious Mr Bedford whose name she has carried for nearly 70 years. The wedding of convenience on 15 November 1935 was arranged with Huxley's help – initially in a facetious spirit with the hunt on for a suitable 'bugger' who would make himself scarce once the deed was done. (The story is told in unpublished letters which sit, like so much vital Huxley material, in the archives, this time in Cambridge.) 'She has married her postman,' Virginia Woolf erroneously noted in her diary. In fact, Walter Croan, 'otherwise Walter Bedford' (as the marriage certificate filled out at the City of Westminster registry office describes him) was a 40-year-old attendant at a gentleman's club in St James's, living at 154 Warwick Street, SW1. Not – as the anonymous *Daily Telegraph* obituarist would gallantly write after Sybille's death – 'a British Army officer'. His 24-year-old bride, Sybille von Schoenebeck, daughter of Maximilian Josef von Schoenebeck (deceased; profession declared as a man of 'independent means') gave her address as the Albany. Huxley and Pierre Mimerel were the two witnesses. She never spoke publicly of this event and no one dared raise it.

19 April 2002: London

The reviews have been nicer to me than to Huxley who clearly retains the power to upset certain kinds of English opinion. Some of them are quite vicious about him.

A small envelope arrives this morning via my publisher bearing the red crest of the House of Lords. I tear open the envelope and read a single sentence in the centre of the expanse of cream paper.

'Dear Mr Murray. I have just read your *Aldous Huxley*, and think it one of the best literary biographies I have ever encountered. Yours sincerely, Roy Jenkins.'

Perhaps Aldous Huxley has more admirers than I think.

25 April 2002: Chelsea, Old Church Street

Sybille has now finished my book and wants to talk to me about it. When I arrive, since she has been so kind about it I press her a little to see if she has found any errors. She says that I was wrong to describe the triangle as a *ménage à trois* since the three never actually lived together. It was more of an affair conducted clandestinely over a period of time. We sip our wine and she reveals (later saying that she did not tell me this before because she felt I was an unknown quantity but now she could trust me) that the relationship that did merit that description was the one between Maria, Aldous and Costanza da Fasola. In my book I describe how Maria and Costanza, the Italian countess, lived together at Forte before Aldous's marriage (swimming naked together, sending a photograph of Maria in the buff to Lady Ottoline, a snap that languishes in a cardboard file in Texas) but Sybille explained (a fact never revealed before) that Aldous was also Costanza's lover (a fact that had not been known to me before). One night Costanza would sleep with Maria, the next with Aldous. She wants me to know this she says because she is probably the only person alive who does know about it and she wants someone to know. And now they do. And does it matter? This relationship persisted through the Italian years – at Forte and Florence – and probably lasted until Costanza's death.

Sybille also demurs at my description of Maria as 'bisexual' (in fact, I had quoted Sybille herself in a newspaper interview using this term). She says simply: 'Maria was homosexual.' She had no interest in men and did not have affairs with them. She implies that even the birth of Matthew was an achievement. But then, in apparent contradiction, she said that Aldous was 'very careless' and, in spite of knowing that doctors had told Maria that it was not safe for her to have another child she did become pregnant. Several times in the 1930s Maria had to return from Sanary to London clinics ('not quite back street abortions') to have abortions while Sybille kept house in her absence at their home in Sanary, La Gorguette.

Sybille is clearly upset at the hostility evinced by many reviewers towards Huxley and their refusal either to read my book or, more widely, to discuss his ideas about the future of mankind and to recognise his overall achievement.

She returns, yet again, to Laura, prompted by the fact that she has been thanked as a source by me. I explain, however, that I got very little out of her and likewise from Matthew, though he was a delightful man. She makes dark references to Huxley's will and Matthew's share of it.

She says that the parts of my book she liked most were those where I had dealt with Huxley's ideas and philosophy – she was particularly complimentary about my chapter on *Eyeless in Gaza* – and wonders whether I would really have preferred to concentrate on those elements rather than going through all the details of the life again: 'That was why your book on Bruce Chatwin was so good.' I think that she is disappointed by the inability of contemporary critics to get to grips with Huxley's ideas.

We drink a glass of dry white wine during this discussion and, although it is a sunny day, the lighting in the ground floor flat is distinctly subfusc. I can hear footsteps in the flat above. There are copies of Auden's poems, and some writings of Henry James on her writing desk. She says it is difficult to write as she can't type now – 'I always find writing very difficult'. On another book-table my biography lies on top of *Painted Shadow* by Carole Seymour-Jones whom I met on a rainy day in Cambridge where we were the sole occupants of the modern archives that morning. There are a great many empty bottles of wine neatly arranged about the flat.

Just before arriving I had found, in a Red Cross charity shop at the end of her street, a first edition of Sybille's book *As it was*. I asked them for a rubber to erase the price (£1.75) and now I produce it at the end when she has become 'dizzy' and wants me to go. I say I will bring it on another occasion but she insists on signing it, only worrying that her condition will prevent her from 'writing something nice'. At her desk she brightens up and signs it:

'NICHOLAS
with much good will
Sybille
and approval
London April 2002'

There is a wry little chuckle from behind the desk over that 'approval'. She says we should keep in touch and seems very interested that I was doing a talk at the Hampstead and Highgate Festival in May. She is clearly interested in the reception of the book and how it bears on Huxley's current reputation. Earlier, she has referred to the political crisis in France (the defeat of the socialist presidential candidate by Le Pen) and chuckles that 'the Socialists will now have to vote for the Conservatives'. As I leave she closes the door quickly, obviously not well in spite of the pill she has just taken.

Once again I hear the mortise locks being turned noisily one by one as they were when I first rang the bell.

I will never see her again.

19 December 2003: London

Sybille rings after having been sent by her old editor at Collins, Richard Ollard, a copy of an article I have written in the *Guardian* about what it is like to write a biography in the shadow of a legendary precursor. She likes it but wants to say that she was not an 'authorised' biographer and had worked out a complicated contract which prevented people from changing anything.

She says we live in a 'very very painful world' now and she is quite pessimistic about the future. She has been quite unwell and is struggling with her book, which will now be shorter and not cover the period when she was writing the Huxley biography.

She remains puzzled at one of the Huxley biographical cruces: his refusal to face the facts of Maria's illness. She thinks it was the shock of his mother's death and the suicide of his brother, Trev, and fear about the threat to his own eyes.

Yet again, she says she had half-hoped that I wouldn't go in to the sexual matters but at the same time she accepts that I had no choice.

She also says there are things that haven't come out and shouldn't.

She says she is in receipt of money from the Royal Literary Fund and her books don't sell.

She concludes that the Huxleys had provided her with 'a moral education' for she has not had a conventional one – which is why she cannot spell.

9 June 2004: London

A brief phone message from Sybille just after she has had a visit from Aldous's son, Matthew, and his wife. I met them on 27 May in the Great Court of the British Museum where they were having lunch with friends in the top floor restaurant. I try to suggest delicately that they should donate Aldous's letters to Matthew to the British Library, an idea that seems to appeal to them. I seem not to have kept a record of Sybille's message so it can't have been important. On Monday 14 February 2005 I receive an email from Franziska Huxley to say that Matthew has died. I mention this to Hilary Spurling when I meet her ten days later at a Royal Literary Fund meeting in Birmingham where we are sitting next to each other at dinner. She says that Sybille's Huxley biography is seriously over-rated: 'She hasn't got a biographical bone in her body.' Hilary says this with such a sweet smile that it isn't until much later that I realise how devastating the comment is – and how much I disagree with it.

25th July 2005: Wales

A call from Sybille to my Wales number. She has just received a postcard from me in which I said how much I had enjoyed *Quicksands*. The postcard shows my house, a white cottage on the side of a hill, which she says looks very attractive. I had concluded my note with: 'Write some more.' She says she has been 'touched' by my card. I too am touched that I should have been the recipient of such unforced generosity and 'kindness' from this remarkable woman. Her voice sounds very frail. She hints that because of medical problems she might soon have to leave her flat.

I never hear from her again.

5 June 2006, London

I arrive at the Reform Club in Pall Mall, barbarously without a tie, to 'a celebration of the life of Sybille Bedford'. The head porter, alarmed but not unprepared, dives below his counter and produces a carrier bag full of ties and instructs one of his lackeys to guide me towards the Gentlemen's lavatory where I will find a tall mahogany pier glass to aid me in my quick change of appearance from lout to toff. I am just finishing off the (rather loud) tie when an impeccably dressed man of my own age emerges from the deeper interior of the lavatory complex. I recognise him as the former Poetry Editor of the *Times Literary Supplement* who, two decades ago, used to commission me, on exquisitely handwritten little white postcards, to write reviews of new verse but he is of course much more famous now for his Booker Prize-winning novel, just televised, *The Line of Beauty*.

Hollinghurst approves the tie and says of course he remembers me though we have only ever communicated by letter. He purrs suavely: 'How pleasant to meet in the lavatory of the Reform Club.'

Nicholas Murray is the biographer of Bruce Chatwin (1993), Matthew Arnold (1996), Aldous Huxley (*An English Intellectual*: 2002), and Franz Kafka (2004). His latest book is a collection of poetry: *The Narrators* (2006).

Letters

Nein!

Unreserved compliments for the new issue of *Areté* (Issue 19) and just a few extremely *besserwisserische* remarks by a German who claims to know better how it is, regarding Michael Hofmann's translations from German.

p 134 Roth's first essay, 'Spaziergang': *der lächerlich unscheinbare Zug*. 'Zug' in this context derives from drawing, not from 'pull tension, force', the *Züge eines Gesichtes* are the features an artist would have drawn in a portrait.

p 135 *Die Romantik der Kaschemmennächte bricht*: I'd have to check again, not having the book at hand, but I'm almost sure the simile intended is that of a wave breaking

p 135 Again *Zug* or *Züge*, here: *Fronleichnamszüge des Patriotismus*: you're patently correct about the Christian calendar but one has to add that the word 'celebrations' is far too weak to capture the demonstrative effect and intention of the traditional *Fronleichnamsprozession* which showed the Catholic forces in all their might and splendour. Martin Luther condemned the processions as the most despicable display of Catholic arrogance, over centuries they played an important part in the cultural struggle between Catholics and Protestants.

The *Zug* or the *Züge* must smack of marches, hence the close connection to Patriotismus.

137 *Und Machorkarauch stieg aus dem plumpen Turm*: why 'turrets' in Hofmann's original if the German original only speaks of one? p137 *Wie der Gekreuzigte lag dieser Frosch*: I don't think the word 'someone' in Hofmann is adequate, it's clearly Christ, the Crucified.

Yours ever,
Tilman Spengler

Nay!

You rightly point (Issue 19, p 135) that Michael Hofmann mistranslates *Fronleichnamszüge* as 'Ascension Day celebrations'. However you follow this with a solecism of your own. Corpus Christi, the Thursday after Trinity Sunday, does not 'coincide with' Maundy Thursday, the Thursday before Easter. They are nine weeks apart.

Yours faithfully,
Michael Frost

Two Left Feet

I very much enjoyed James Womack's article on Tom Paulin (Issue 19), but on page 153 he has seriously nodded off: 'For example, in W H Auden's *Letter to Lord Byron*, the line "And all the spicier bits of Anthropology" is a regular iambic pentameter.' Crikey, it's no such thing. I agree that 'spicier' is not a dactyl, but with the final foot x/xx how can it possibly be 'a regular iambic pentameter'? No amount of funny or strained pronunciation can make it one.

Very best wishes,
Bernard Richards

Areté writes: No fault attaches to Mr Womack. For reasons too tedious to explain, the mistake is ours. We can't count. The line is an iambic hexameter.

Back Issues

Issue 1 T S Eliot – unpublished letters to James Joyce, Ezra Pound, Virginia Woolf & W B Yeats / Patrick Marber – *Casting* / New fiction by Ian McEwan and Peter Ho Davies / A prose poem by Harold Pinter / *A la recherche du temps perdu* – Craig Raine

Issue 2 William Golding – *Scenes from a Life*, an unpublished memoir / Julian Barnes and Rose Tremain – new fiction / Martin Amis and Ian McEwan on Borges / Christopher Logue on visiting Brecht

Issue 3 Boris Pasternak – Letters from a Marriage / Ralph Fiennes on acting Shakespeare / David Lodge – new fiction / Reviews by Frederic Raphael and Tilman Spengler / Christopher Reid – *Eating Out*, three poems

Issue 4 Martin Amis on literary criticism / Adam Thorpe – *Towards a Little Theatre* / James Fenton – seven songs / Colin Matthews – *Diary of a Composition*

Issue 5 Scenes from Harold Pinter's screenplay of *Lolita* / An interview with David Lodge / Blake Morrison on song lyrics / Reportage by Peter Foster and Dorothy Gallagher

Issue 6 Christopher Logue – *All Day Permanent Red*, new versions from Homer / John Haffenden – William Empson in Japan / William Boyd – *The Eleven Year War* / Peter Morris – *The Age of Consent* / Simon Armitage – three poems

Issue 7 Bella Freud – *The Art of Fashion* / David Hare – *The Art of Lying* / Philip Gosse – *Cancer: A Memoir* / Matthew Leeming in Afghanistan / Sex, drugs & alcohol in Iran

Issue 8 Julian Barnes on syphilis / Patrick Marber's *Late One Night* / New fiction by Panos Karnezis / An Interview with Enno Patalas

Issue 9 Ian McEwan on Love and Death / Ben Rice's first film script / August Kleinzahler on Ginsberg / New fiction by Philippa Stockley

Issue 10 Fiction by Adam Thirlwell / Interviews with Orhan Pamuk and Pawel Pawlikowski / A masterpiece by Dorothy Nimmo / Frederic Raphael on Stanley Kubrick

Issue 11 Tom Stoppard's unpublished screenplay – *Galileo*

Issue 12 Kipling's unpublished motoring diaries / Pasternak's unpublished suicide letter / Matthew Norman is stabbed in South Africa / Adam Thirlwell on Sebald / Craig Raine on Lowell

Issue 13 Unpublished poems by Vladimir Nabokov / *Pleas and Directions*, a play by Patrick Malahide / Interview with Christopher Logue

Issue 14 Evelyn Waugh on Hollywood / A radio play by Patrick Marber / William Boyd – a story / Harold Pinter on *Waiting for Godot*

Issue 15 Ian McEwan interviews John Updike / Peter Nichols's *Diaries* / Ann Pasternak Slater: *The Case of Rudolf Kasztner* / The genius of Richard van den Dool

Issue 16 William Golding – unpublished journals / Richard Eyre interviews Trevor Griffiths / Peter Nichols in New York / The reputations of Isaac Bashevis Singer, Philip Roth, Pablo Neruda, Marianne Moore.

Issue 17 *Longing* – A Play by William Boyd / Interview with Mark Alexander / Fiction by Panos Karnezis and Julie Maxwell / Reviews of Ishiguro, Akhmatova, Robert Lowell, Geoffrey Hill, Seamus Heaney, Christopher Logue.

Issue 18 Homage to Joe Brainard: Patrick Marber, Ann Robinson, Sue Townsend, David Lodge, Wendy Cope, Harriet Walter, Dorothy Gallagher, Paul Farley, Josephine Hart, Ben Rice, David Mitchell, Michael Lesslie

Issue 19 Frances Stonor Saunders – The Woman who Shot Mussolini / Veronica Horwell in Bosnia and the USA / Christopher Reid's great elegy / The Mother of a Murdered Prostitute: An Interview

UK – £7.99 each, plus £1 p&p per copy. Europe – 16 Euros. USA/Australia/New Zealand – $18.
Please make cheques payable to 'Areté Magazine', 8 New College Lane, Oxford, OX1 3BN.

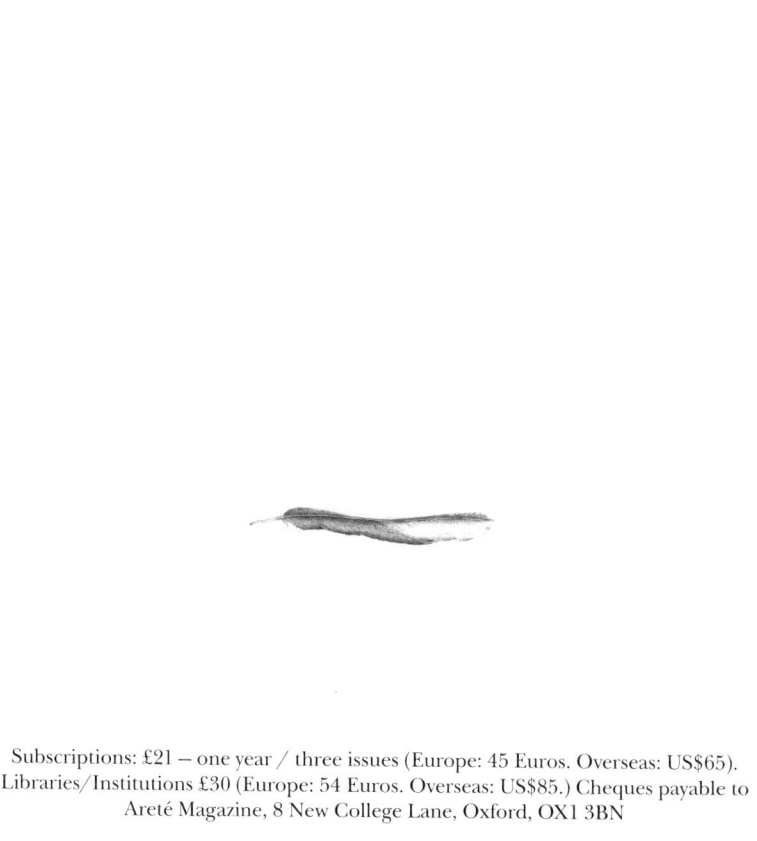

Subscriptions: £21 – one year / three issues (Europe: 45 Euros. Overseas: US$65).
Libraries/Institutions £30 (Europe: 54 Euros. Overseas: US$85.) Cheques payable to
Areté Magazine, 8 New College Lane, Oxford, OX1 3BN

Culture seeks to do away with classes. The great men of culture have laboured to divest knowledge of all that was harsh, uncouth, difficult, abstract, professional, exclusive; to humanise it, to make it efficient outside the clique of the cultivated and learned.

Matthew Arnold· *Culture & Anarchy*